RAND NATIONAL SECURITY RESEARCH DIVISION

Out of the Shadows

The Health and Well-Being of Private Contractors Working in Conflict Environments

Molly Dunigan, Carrie M. Farmer, Rachel M. Burns, Alison Hawks, Claude Messan Setodji

This report is a product of the RAND Corporation's continuing program of self-initiated independent research. Support for such research is provided, in part, by donors and by the independent research and development provisions of RAND's contracts for the operation of its U.S. Department of Defense federally funded research and development centers. The research was conducted within the RAND National Security Research Division of the RAND Corporation.

Library of Congress Cataloging-in-Publication Data is available for this publication.

ISBN: 978-0-8330-8233-6

The RAND Corporation is a nonprofit institution that helps improve policy and decisionmaking through research and analysis. RAND's publications do not necessarily reflect the opinions of its research clients and sponsors.

Support RAND—make a tax-deductible charitable contribution at www.rand.org/giving/contribute.html

RAND® is a registered trademark.

Cover image by Shutterstock

RAND OFFICES

SANTA MONICA, CA • WASHINGTON, DC

PITTSBURGH, PA • NEW ORLEANS, LA • JACKSON, MS • BOSTON, MA

DOHA, QA • CAMBRIDGE, UK • BRUSSELS, BE

www.rand.org

Preface

Over the past decade, private contractors have been deployed extensively around the globe. In addition to supporting U.S. and allied forces in Iraq and Afghanistan, they have assisted foreign governments, nongovernmental organizations, and private businesses by providing a wide range of services, including base support and maintenance, logistical support, transportation, intelligence, communication, construction, and security.

Contractors working in conflict environments are exposed to many of the same combat stressors as military personnel. These stressors are known to have physical and mental health implications, and there has been much research on the causes and consequences of combat and operational stress among military personnel. Yet, despite anecdotal evidence of similar problems among contractors, there has been very little study of this issue to date.

This report presents findings from a RAND study that attempted to bridge this research gap by estimating the prevalence of mental and physical health challenges across a large sample of contractors working in conflict environments and by identifying the extent to which contractors use health care services, as well as the barriers and facilitators to receiving care.

This report is a product of the RAND Corporation's continuing program of self-initiated independent research. Support for such research is provided, in part, by donors and by the independent research and development provisions of RAND's contracts for the operation of its U.S. Department of Defense federally funded research and development centers. The research was conducted within the RAND National Security Research Division (NSRD) of the RAND Corporation. NSRD conducts research and analysis on defense and national security topics for the U.S. and allied defense, foreign policy, homeland security, and intelligence communities and foundations and other nongovernmental organizations that support defense and national security analysis.

For more information on the RAND National Security Research Division, see http://www.rand.org/nsrd.html or contact the director (contact information is provided on the web page).

Contents

Figures

Tables

Summary

Over the past decade, private contractors have been deployed extensively to conflict environments around the globe. In addition to supporting U.S. and allied forces in Iraq and Afghanistan, contractors have assisted foreign governments, nongovernmental organizations, and private businesses by providing a wide range of services, including base support and maintenance, logistical support, transportation, intelligence, communication, construction, and security. While exact numbers of contractors employed by various entities in conflict environments internationally are unknown, contractors employed by the U.S. Department of Defense (DoD) at the height of the conflicts in Iraq and Afghanistan outnumbered U.S. troops deployed to both theaters: For example, DoD employed 155,826 contractors alongside 152,275 U.S. troops in Iraq in 2008 and 94,413 contractors alongside 91,600 U.S. troops in Afghanistan in 2010 (Sié Chéou-Kang Center for International Security and Diplomacy, 2013). Such figures may not provide a true gauge of the industry's size, however, nor are they necessarily representative of future contractor deployments.

Although these contractors are not supposed to engage in offensive combat, they may nonetheless be exposed to such stressors as gunfire, improvised explosive devices (IEDs), and other modes of attack; serious injury; kidnapping; the deaths of fellow personnel; and the psychological aftermath of killing. These stressors are known to have physical and mental health implications for military personnel: It is estimated that 5–20 percent of U.S. service members returning from deployments suffer from post-traumatic stress disorder (PTSD) (Ramchand et al., 2010), with lower rates of PTSD among service members from other nations (for example, the rate is estimated to be 3–7 percent among UK personnel; see Engelhard et al., 2007; Iversen et al., 2009; Richardson, Frueh, and Acierno, 2010; and Fear et al., 2010). Yet, despite anecdotal evidence of similar problems among contractors, there has been very little study of this issue to date.

This report attempts to fill that void by presenting results from a RAND research study that explored the prevalence and nature of health problems among the deployed contractor population. Building on prior research on military mental health and wartime contracting, the study addressed two related questions:

1. What is the prevalence of mental and physical health problems among contractors who have deployed at least once to a theater of conflict in the 2011–2013 time frame?
2. To what extent do contractors who work in conflict environments use mental health care services, and what are the barriers and facilitators to receiving care?

Survey Approach

RAND conducted an online survey of 660 contractors who had deployed on contract to a theater of conflict at least once in the previous two years (early 2011 through early 2013). Two-thirds (61 percent) of respondents were U.S. citizens, 24 percent were UK citizens, and the rest were citizens of Australia, South Africa, New Zealand, or other nations. The majority (84 percent) had previously served in the armed forces. The largest proportion of respondents (38 percent) were engaged in land security services, including convoy security, static site security, and personal security details, during their contracts. The remaining proportion of respondents were engaged in transportation, training or advising, maritime security, base support, logistics, management, or other services during their contracts.

In addition to gathering demographic and employment information, the survey asked respondents about their deployment experience (including level of preparation for deployment, combat exposure, and living conditions), their mental health (including criteria for probable PTSD, depression, and high-risk alcohol use), their physical health, and their access to and use of health care. The purpose was to identify contractors' levels health and well-being and to explore differences by such factors as country of citizenship, job specialty, and length and frequency of deployment.

Major Findings

Contractor Deployment Experiences Vary with Their Circumstances

Deployment experiences likely play a role in shaping the health and well-being of contractors. We found that contractors' levels of deployment preparedness and combat exposure were roughly similar to those of military populations. Contractors' living conditions (e.g., access to clean clothing, ability to get sufficient sleep, access to means to communicate with friends and family) were better than those reported by a sample of Gulf War veterans (King et al., 2006), and contractor deployment preparation was slightly better than that of U.S. Army medics (Chapman et al., 2012). However, there were some notable differences among the contractors surveyed:

- UK citizens reported better preparation, lower levels of combat exposure, and better living conditions than U.S. citizens, on average. However, citizens of coun-

tries other than the United States and the United Kingdom reported even better experiences in these categories.
- Transportation contractors reported the lowest levels of preparation, the highest combat exposure, and the worst living conditions of all job specialties. Logistics/maintenance contractors fared best in all three categories, and maritime security contractors fared equally to logistics/maintenance contractors in terms of combat exposure and living conditions.
- Contractors with shorter, more-frequent deployments reported higher levels of preparedness than those with longer, less-frequent deployments. Shorter deployments were also correlated with lower combat exposure and better living conditions.
- Contractors who carried a weapon felt better prepared for deployment than those who did not.

Contractors Are Affected by Serious Mental Health Problems

The survey found that the proportion of respondents with mental health problems was at least as great as that in military populations:

- Twenty-five percent of contractors met criteria for probable PTSD. Moreover, 18 percent screened positive for depression, and 10 percent reported high-risk drinking. By comparison, the respective proportions of U.S. military troops deployed to Iraq or Afghanistan have been estimated at 4–20 percent for PTSD, 5–37 percent for depression, and 4.7–39 percent for alcohol abuse (Institute of Medicine, 2013). Rates of PTSD are lower among UK military personnel, with 4–7 percent reporting probable PTSD. However, the prevalence of other mental health problems among UK service members is similar to that among the contractors we surveyed, with 20 percent of UK military personnel reporting symptoms of common mental disorders, such as depression, and 13–67 percent reporting alcohol abuse (Fear et al., 2010, 2007).
- Transportation contractors showed the highest rate of probable PTSD (50 percent), most likely due to greater combat exposure than other job specialties (as noted earlier).[1]
- U.S. contractors reported more mental health problems than UK contractors: Thirty-two percent of U.S. contractors met criteria for probable PTSD (compared with 12 percent of UK contractors), and 23 percent of U.S. contractors met criteria for depression (compared with 9 percent of UK contractors). The difference may be due to cultural or societal differences in the experience of traumatic events or in the reporting of mental health symptoms. U.S. military personnel also

[1] It should be noted, however, that the size of our sample of transportation contractors was relatively small. This finding therefore speaks to the need for further research specifically on the health needs of the population of contractors engaged in transportation services.

experience higher rates of PTSD than do military personnel from other Western nations (Richardson, Frueh, and Acierno, 2010).
- Longer deployments and increased combat exposure were each associated with higher rates of PTSD and depression. Increased preparedness was associated with lower rates of mental health problems. Similarly, combat-exposed UK military personnel have reported higher rates of PTSD compared with those who were not exposed to combat (Fear et al., 2010).

Contractors Also Suffer from Physical Health Problems

In addition to mental health stressors, contractors may be exposed to physical health dangers, ranging from respiratory problems to serious, life-changing injuries. The survey asked respondents to assess their overall health, to report whether they had ever been diagnosed with a traumatic brain injury (TBI), and to describe any other health problems they believed they suffered as a result of their deployment on contract. Major findings are as follows:

- The majority of respondents said that they were in "excellent" or "very good" health. Ten percent had been diagnosed with a TBI at some point in their lives. Thirty-nine percent reported other health problems (most frequently, respiratory issues, back pain, and hearing problems) that they believed they had acquired from their contract deployment.
- Health problems varied considerably between contractors from different countries. Fifty-three percent of U.S. contractors reported suffering from a physical health condition due to their contracted deployment, compared with only 16 percent of UK contractors. The discrepancy holds true even after controlling for other factors, such as combat exposure, length of deployment, and mental health issues. The underlying reason deserves further examination.
- Health problems also varied by job specialty. Transportation contractors were most likely to report a physical health condition (55 percent), and maritime security contractors were least likely (15 percent).
- Respondents working on contracts funded by DoD or the U.S. Department of State (DoS) were more likely to report a physical health problem than were those working on other contracts. The rate of health problems was equal for DoD- and DoS-funded contractors.
- On average, those who reported physical health problems also had higher combat exposure, were more likely to meet criteria for probable PTSD, and had higher rates of depression.

Most Contractors Have Health Insurance, but Not All Health Care Needs Are Being Met

Having identified significant instances of physical and mental health problems among contractors, we next sought to determine whether contractors were seeking and receiving treatment. We asked respondents about their access to health insurance during and after deployment, whether they had filed claims under the Defense Base Act (DBA), and whether they had sought treatment for mental health issues during the previous year (and if not, why not). Our primary conclusions are as follows:

- Eighty-three percent of contractors surveyed had health insurance at the time of the survey, but there were differences from country to country. The proportion of U.S. contractors without health insurance was 21 percent, compared with 12 percent for UK contractors and 10 percent for those who were citizens of other countries. Eighty percent of respondents reported receiving health insurance from their contracting firm while they were deployed, but this was mostly limited to the deployment period or to a short time afterward.
- Only 16 percent of contractors sampled had ever made a DBA claim. Among those whose most recent contract had been funded by the U.S. government, 22 percent reported that they had made a DBA claim. The DBA mandates that all civilian employees working outside the United States on U.S. military bases or under a contract with the U.S. government for public works or national defense have access to workers' compensation for injuries or deaths sustained as a result of such employment. We found that, among respondents who applied for benefits, 57 percent of claims were approved and 37 percent were either denied or still being processed at the time of the survey. (Six percent of respondents reported that they did not know the outcome of their DBA claim.) Contractors from the United States were more likely to file DBA claims than those from other countries.
- There is a significant unmet need for health care, with only 28 percent of those with probable PTSD and 34 percent of those with probable depression receiving mental health treatment in the 12 months prior to the survey. This may be due to the perceived stigma of having a mental health problem or other barriers to receiving mental health care; contractors with probable PTSD or depression were twice as likely to report barriers to receiving mental health treatment, including cost, embarrassment, and concerns about being perceived as weak.

Recommendations

The survey results suggest that deployments to combat theaters place significant stresses on contractors, with implications for both physical and mental health. Mental health problems, especially probable PTSD and depression, are of particular concern, and many contractors are not getting the treatment they need. The following recommendations suggest how private companies, government entities, and the research community can help address these needs.

Increase Access to Stress Management and Mental Health Resources

Contractors receive infrequent training in stress management prior to a combat deployment, and there are few company-provided resources available during or after a combat deployment. We found that when such resources were available, instances of probable PTSD and depression were much lower. Private contracting firms employing these contractors—including but not limited to private military and security companies, risk consultancies, development companies, and construction and engineering companies, logistics firms, and transportation companies—should consider providing these resources more uniformly. In addition, funding agents that issue these contracts, such as DoD, might consider requiring that contractor personnel have access to stress and mental health resources as a condition of the contract.

Reduce the Stigma in Seeking Treatment for Mental Health Problems

The perceived stigma associated with mental health care is a significant barrier to contractors who need such care. Research on stigma reduction suggests that programs that provide education about mental health problems and contact with people who have been treated for mental health problems have been successful in reducing stigma (Collins et al., 2012; Penn and Couture, 2002; Thornicroft et al., 2008). To encourage greater usage of mental health care among those who need it, companies could implement programs to increase awareness about stress and mental health problems associated with contract deployments, train team leaders to identify and normalize stress reactions, and provide access to confidential counseling.

Conduct Additional Research to Better Understand the Needs of This Population

This research is intended as an exploratory study of the physical and mental health issues that affect contractors and the factors that facilitate or impede their treatment. Understanding the causes behind the results documented here will help policymakers and private companies take steps to improve the health and well-being of contractors. Additional research is therefore needed in the following areas:

- understanding how predeployment readiness training can protect contractors from deployment-related health conditions
- shaping deployment experiences to improve contractors' health and well-being
- developing a deeper understanding of the physical health problems that contractors face and any barriers to care (as a counterpart to this study's focus on mental health)
- investigating the reasons why contractors from different countries have different outcomes in many areas addressed in this study
- surveying a larger population of contractors in specific job specialties of interest, such as transportation and logistics/maintenance

- extending the scope of this analysis to contractors deployed over the past decade (and thus encompassing deployments as far back as the early years of both Iraq and Afghanistan).

Acknowledgments

We gratefully acknowledge the assistance of a number of individuals, organizations, and companies that helped us develop the survey and disseminate it to as many contractors as possible. Although we cannot name them publicly, we are grateful for their assistance. At RAND, we thank Anna Smith for her administrative support in preparing this document, Robert Guffey for his writing support, and Lauren Skrabala for her skillful assistance in editing the document. We also thank Joshua Breslau, Jennifer Cerully, and Mark Sorbero for their writing and research assistance. We owe Sean McFate a debt of gratitude for sharing his knowledge with us throughout the course of this research. We are also incredibly appreciative of the valuable insights we received from Neil Greenberg and Margaret Harrell. Their constructive critiques were addressed as part of RAND's rigorous quality assurance process to improve the quality of this report. Susan Marquis, Richard Neu, and the RAND-Initiated Research program deserve special thanks for funding this research. Finally, we thank all of the contractors who completed the survey, both for their time and for their valuable input.

Abbreviations

AUDIT-C	Alcohol Use Disorders Identification Test–Consumption
CI	confidence interval
DBA	Defense Base Act
DoD	U.S. Department of Defense
DoS	U.S. Department of State
DRRI	Deployment Risk and Resilience Inventory
FY	fiscal year
IED	improvised explosive device
MTF	military treatment facility
NGO	nongovernmental organization
OEF	Operation Enduring Freedom
OIF	Operation Iraqi Freedom
OR	odds ratio
PCL-C	PTSD Checklist–Civilian Version
PHQ-2	Patient Health Questionnaire–2
PSC	private security contractor
PTSD	posttraumatic stress disorder
std	standard deviation
TBI	traumatic brain injury

CHAPTER ONE

Introduction

Private contractors have been deployed extensively over the past decade to support U.S. and coalition operations in both Iraq and Afghanistan, at times outnumbering U.S. troops in these theaters. Although contractor deployments have received a substantial amount of media, scholarly, and government attention throughout this period, contractors are often referred to in the literature as a "shadow force" (see, for instance, Isenberg, 2008), operating below the radar or in the shadows of their military counterparts. Nonetheless, contractors support numerous other entities beyond U.S. and allied forces in Iraq, Afghanistan, and elsewhere around the globe, including foreign governments, nongovernmental organizations (NGOs), and private businesses. Contractors provide a variety of services under these contracts, ranging from base support and maintenance (including such tasks as sanitation, laundry, and food services) to logistical support, transportation, intelligence, communication, construction, and various types of security (including personal security details, convoy security, and static site security).

Scholarly and media attention devoted to this industry over the past decade has focused primarily on the rise of the industry and its political and economic effects, issues of contractor accountability and potential regulatory mechanisms, whether the industry represents an abrogation of state sovereignty, contractor interactions with professional militaries and their effects on military effectiveness, contractors' impact on local civilians and their communities in the theaters in which they operate, and policy-oriented government reports detailing the extent and nature of contractor operations in certain theaters during specific time frames.

Coverage of individual contractor experiences and well-being has been less prevalent. Yet, because contractors deploy to the same theaters as state militaries, it is reasonable to question whether individual contractors might be exposed to similar combat stresses. Studies suggest that the prevalence of posttraumatic stress disorder (PTSD) is in the range of 5–20 percent among U.S. troops returning from Operation Enduring Freedom (OEF) and Operation Iraqi Freedom (OIF) combat deployment, with variations due to differences in how the population is defined and which measures are used (Ramchand et al., 2010). Studies of PTSD among troops from the United Kingdom and other coalition partners have generally found a lower but still worrying prevalence of PTSD (Sundin et al., 2010) and other mental health problems, such as alcohol abuse (Fear et al., 2010; Rona et al., 2009). A recent UK study found an association between serving in combat in Iraq or Afghanistan and perpetrating violent offenses after returning home—an association attributable, in part, to alcohol misuse and aggressive behavior (MacManus et al., 2013). Given these findings for general populations of coalition troops, it is somewhat surprising that more attention has not been devoted to an examination of the health and well-being of contractors. Although some media reports have highlighted anecdotal evidence that there may be cause for concern regarding the health and well-being of contractors, there have been very few rigorous analyses on this issue to date.

In an effort to bring the health and well-being of deployed contractors out of the shadows, this report details the results of a research study aimed at exploring the prevalence and nature of health problems among the contractor population. It builds upon previous RAND research on military mental health and wartime contracting to address two related questions:

1. What is the prevalence of mental and physical health problems among contractors who have deployed at least once to a theater of conflict in the 2011–2013 time frame?
2. To what extent do contractors who work in conflict environments use mental health care services, and what are the barriers and facilitators to receiving care?

To address these questions, RAND launched a survey in February 2013 aimed broadly at the transnational population of individuals who had deployed on contract to a theater of conflict at least once in the previous two years (early 2011 through early 2013). The private contracting industry is highly fluid, with people entering and exiting at a constant pace; we limited the survey to those who had deployed on contract recently so that we could assess the health and well-being of the *current* and *very recent* contractor workforce.

Nonetheless, it is important to acknowledge that—as is common in survey-based research—some people willing to participate were excluded from doing so. In limiting the study's scope in this manner, we do not discount individuals who deployed on contract prior to the time frame studied. Chapter Two covers much of the relevant literature on contractor health and well-being extending back over the past decade. Moreover, we recognize that the height of wartime contracting in recent years occurred during the 2005–2011 period in both Iraq and Afghanistan, and it is certainly possible that including contractors who deployed during that period would lead us to conclude that the prevalence of health problems among this population is higher than what is reflected in our findings. This study therefore serves as a preliminary examination of this issue and is intended to paint a picture of the current and very recent contractor population, not the entire population of contractors who have served in Iraq, Afghanistan, or elsewhere over the past decade or more.

Our Approach

Description of Survey Sample and Survey Recruitment

Private contractors working in conflict environments are a diverse group, with individuals working as independent agents on contracts sponsored by a variety of government and nongovernmental entities and for an unknown number of contracting firms. While the exact number of contractors employed annually by various entities in conflict environments around the globe is unknown, contractors employed by the U.S. Department of Defense (DoD) at the height of the conflicts in Iraq and Afghanistan outnumbered U.S. troops deployed to both theaters. For example, DoD employed 155,826 contractors alongside 152,275 U.S. troops in Iraq in 2008 and 94,413 contractors alongside 91,600 U.S. troops in Afghanistan in 2010 (Sié Chéou-Kang Center for International Security and Diplomacy, 2013). Such figures may not provide a true gauge of the industry's size, however, as they do not include the number of contractors working in conflict environments for private business entities, NGOs, foreign governments, or even other U.S. government agencies. Nor should these figures be considered representative of future contractor deployments; the conflicts in Iraq and Afghanistan caused widespread expansion in the industry that may or may not be replicated in the future.

As such, there is no reasonable sampling frame for the entire population of contractors if one wanted to extend the analysis beyond contractors employed by a single company or members of a single trade association. Moreover, contractors who work in conflict environments are a hard-to-reach population. To overcome these population sampling challenges, our survey relied on a large, transnational convenience sample of such contractors.[1] We distributed the survey's web link as widely as possible through several large contracting firms and trade associations based in the United States, the United Kingdom, and elsewhere, as well as via email listservs and web forums targeted to the contractor population, social networking sites, and personal networks. We also used snowball sampling, asking those who responded to the survey to forward the link to other eligible contractors.

Due to this effort to expand the reach of the survey beyond a single company or national trade association, and to therefore gain information on a broader and more diverse sample of contractors than is commonly found in other survey-based studies of this population, it is impossible to know the total number of individuals who would have been eligible to participate. That said, we were able to compare the characteristics of our sample population with available quantitative data on the global contractor population to assess the extent to which survey respondents were representative of the larger population of contractors operating in conflict environments worldwide.

---

[1] This research was approved by the RAND Human Subjects Protection Committee.

Survey Instrument

The survey assessed demographic and employment characteristics of contractors, including age, citizenship, education, marital status, prior military experience (branch and component of service, length of time in the military, length of separation from the military, rank at separation, number of deployments to a combat zone while in the military, and deployment to Iraq or Afghanistan as part of OIF or OEF), job type during the most recent contract (e.g., base support, personal security detail, logistics), and duration of employment and number of contract deployments with the contractor's current employer.

In the survey, respondents could select more than one job type, since many contractors operate in more than one capacity on a contract. However, for analytical purposes, we recoded these responses so that each respondent was linked to a singular job type. To do this, we used a decision tree, shown in Figure 1.1. Any respondents with multiple job type responses who indicated "transportation" but not "security" were coded as "transportation." From those who were left, any respondents who indicated "training/advising" but not "transportation" were coded as "training/advising." From

Figure 1.1
Job Specialty Recoding Decision Tree

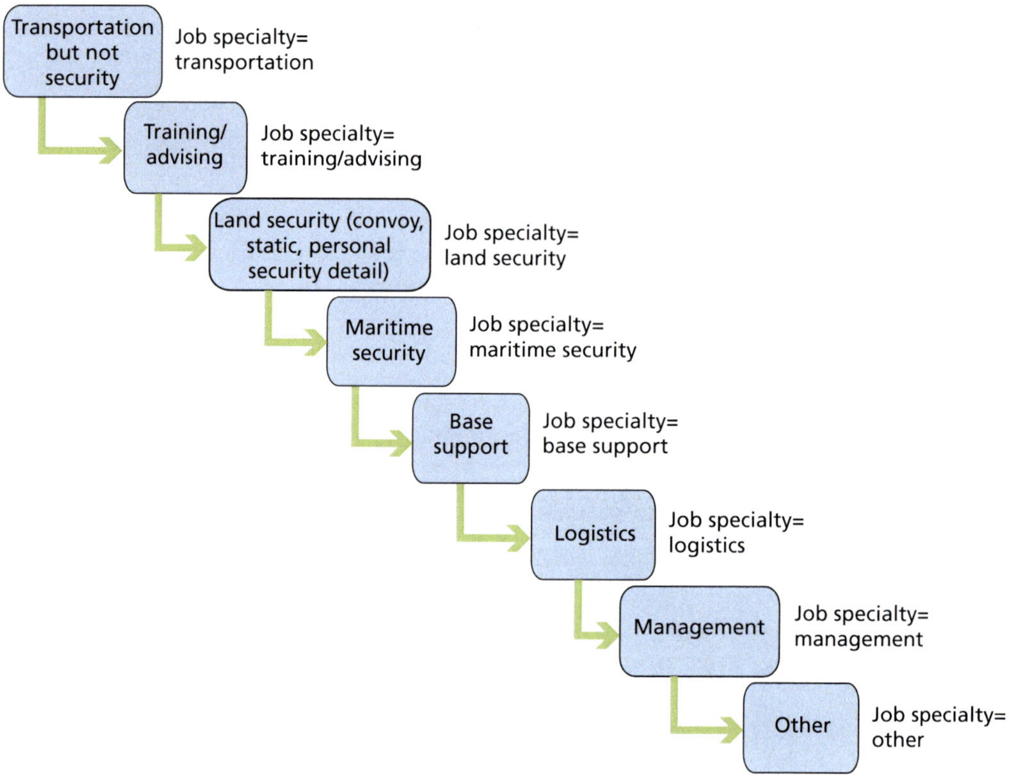

RAND *RR420-1.1*

those who were left, any respondents who indicated land security ("security," "convoy security," "personal security detail," or "static security") and not any of the above were coded as "land security," and any respondents indicating "maritime security" and not any of the above were coded as "maritime security." From those who were left, any respondents who indicated "base support" and not any of the above were coded as "base support"; respondents indicating "logistics" and none of the above were coded as "logistics"; and those indicating "management" and none of the above were coded as "management." Remaining respondents were coded as "other."

The survey also requested information about the most recent contract deployment, such as the contract funder, timing of return from the most recent deployment, and length of the most recent deployment. Respondents were also asked whether they carried a government- or company-issued weapon while deployed on contract.

Respondents were asked to describe their most recent contract deployment using scales modified from the Deployment Risk and Resilience Inventory (DRRI; see King et al., 2006). We modified the DRRI combat exposure scale to reflect contractor experiences more authentically–omitting, for instance, questions about taking part in invasions or assaults on entrenched positions, because contractors, by definition, are not supposed to engage in offensive combat. The modified combat exposure scale included six items with Likert response options, with 1 indicating that the respondent had never experienced the item and 5 indicating that the respondent experienced the item daily during his or her most recent deployment on contract. Scores were calculated by taking an average of all of the items, subtracting one, and multiplying the score by the number of items (six), such that 0 = no combat exposure and 24 = experienced each item every day.

To assess preparation for deployment, we used a slightly modified version of the DRRI preparedness scale. Items on these scales were scored from 1 to 5, with 1 indicating that the individual "strongly disagreed" with the statement and 5 indicating that the individual "strongly agreed" with the statement. These responses were dichotomized so that those agreeing or strongly agreeing with an item received a score of 1 and other responses were coded as 0. The final scale consisted of the average of these items multiplied by the number of items (12) so that the lowest score (0) reflected those who were least prepared and the highest score (12) represented those who were most prepared.

We also somewhat modified the DRRI living conditions scale to more closely reflect contractor experiences. For example, respondents were asked about access to clean clothing, opportunity for privacy, ability to get enough sleep, and exposure to loud noises (see Chapter Three for the full set of items). A response of 1 indicated that an experience occurred "almost none of the time," and a response of 5 indicated that an experience occurred "almost all of the time." Some items were reverse-coded so that higher scores indicated better living conditions. Items were dichotomized so that responses indicating that an experience happened "most of the time" or "almost all of the time" were assigned a score of 1 and the rest received a score of 0. The final scale consisted of the average of these items multiplied by the number of items (17) so that the lowest score (0) reflected those who had the worst living conditions and the highest score (17) represented those who had the best living conditions.

Respondents were asked to assess their overall health status and were provided with a text box in which to provide a short description of any health conditions that they believed were a result of their deployment on contract. We reviewed and categorized these conditions as follows: orthopedic, respiratory, back pain, hearing, PTSD, skin, pain, sleep, stress, anxiety, traumatic brain injury (TBI)/head injury, digestive, vision, cardiac/circulatory, infections/sickness, fatigue/weakness, depression, anger, dental, cancer, diabetes, substance abuse, memory, headache, olfactory, neurological immune system, relationship issues, taste, and leishmaniasis (a disease spread by sand flies). We recoded "other health conditions" to exclude any responses that focused solely on mental health issues (for example, PTSD, depression, or anxiety), because the survey included a number of other questions to assess mental health status separately.

We used the PTSD Checklist–Civilian Version (PCL-C) to assess probable PTSD. Respondents indicated the extent to which they had experienced each of 17 symptoms in the previous month. Using the cluster scoring method, we recorded probable PTSD if respondents reported that they had experienced at least one intrusion symptom, three avoidance symptoms, and two hyperarousal symptoms at least "moderately" over the previous month (Ruggiero et al., 2003). Because there are multiple ways of scoring the PCL-C, we also examined the total score, reporting the proportion of respondents with scores equal to or greater than 30, 44, and 50, which are common cut-points used in military studies.

We used the two-item version of the Patient Health Questionnaire (PHQ-2) to assess probable depression, applying a cut-point of 3 (Löwe, Kroenke, and Gräfe, 2005). The Alcohol Use Disorders Identification Test–Consumption (AUDIT-C) was used to screen for alcohol misuse, defined as an AUDIT-C score of 4 or higher, and high-risk alcohol use, defined as an AUDIT-C score of 8 or higher (Bush et al., 1998). Respondents were also asked about tobacco use and whether a health care provider had ever told them that they had a TBI.

The survey also assessed the health insurance status of respondents, perceived access to company-provided resources for contract-related stress problems, and use of health and mental health care in the previous 12 months. We assessed mental health care stigma in this section of the survey using a scale developed by Hoge and colleagues (2004). We reviewed these items individually. Respondents were then asked about the likelihood of reporting a mental health problem to a supervisor or company official, whether they knew any other contractor who had been diagnosed with a mental health problem, and whether they thought mental health problems were more common among military personnel than among contractors working in theaters of conflict. Respondents were also asked whether they had ever filed a Defense Base Act (DBA) claim, the reason for the claim, and the status of the claim.

Survey Response

The survey was available for 77 days, and in that time, 1,066 people accessed it. Of these, 831 provided informed consent to participate, and 660 met the eligibility criteria for the study. Some of these 660 participants exited the survey before reaching the end. We found no patterns in dropout by contracting specialty, prior military experience, or contracting experience and, therefore, we determined that dropout occurred randomly. For each section of the analysis in the chapters that follow, we use the data from the respondents who completed the relevant items, regardless of whether they completed the full survey.

Survey Analysis

Due to the exploratory nature of this study, most of our analyses consisted of simple univariate measures (means and frequencies) and an assessment of bivariate relationships (chi-square tests, t-tests, and analyses of variance).[2] For example, we explored differences in outcomes by job type, contract funder, citizenship, age, whether the respondent carried a weapon while deployed, previous military experience, length of most recent contract, number of deployments on contract, and combat exposure.

We used logistic regression models to assess the influence of citizenship, combat exposure, job specialty, and previous military experience on rates of PTSD and depression. Odds ratios (ORs) and 95-percent confidence intervals (CIs) are presented in Appendix B.

In light of missing values in the observed data, and in order to account for patterns of missing data (most often toward the end of the survey), we conducted a sensitivity analysis using a multiple imputation procedure (Schafer, 1997). The data were imputed ten times, and the results from each imputed data item were aggregated using standard procedures (Schafer, 1997) and compared to the nonimputed data results where case-wide deletion was considered. The imputed tables can be found in Appendix B.

Overall Sample Characteristics

As discussed in greater detail in Chapter Three, the majority of contractors in our sample (84 percent) had previously served in the armed forces, and 14 percent of this subset had served in the military of a country other than the United States. Many respondents (67 percent) were armed during their most recent deployment on con-

---

[2] All analyses were conducted using SAS version 9.3.

tract.[3] As shown in Figure 1.2, roughly one-third (32 percent) of respondents reported that their most recent contract was funded by DoD, while just over one-fifth (22 percent) worked on a contract funded by the U.S. Department of State (DoS). Of the remainder, most respondents worked on contracts funded by a private business entity (17 percent), a foreign government (10 percent), or a U.S. government agency other than DoD or DoS (7 percent).

As shown in Figure 1.3, the largest proportion of contractors by job specialty had engaged in land security services during their most recent contract, including convoy security, static site security, and personal security details. These contractors, commonly known as private security contractors, or PSCs, accounted for 38 percent of this study's sample. Contractors involved in training and advising military and police forces made up the second-largest group (23 percent of the sample). Maritime security contractors and those falling into the "other" category each made up 10 percent of the sample. Seven percent of respondents performed base support functions, while 6 percent performed management duties. Logistics/maintenance and transportation contractors each accounted for 4 percent of the sample.

As shown in Figure 1.4, 61 percent of respondents were U.S. citizens, and 24 percent were UK citizens. Australians and South Africans each accounted for 4 percent of

Figure 1.2
Contract Funder

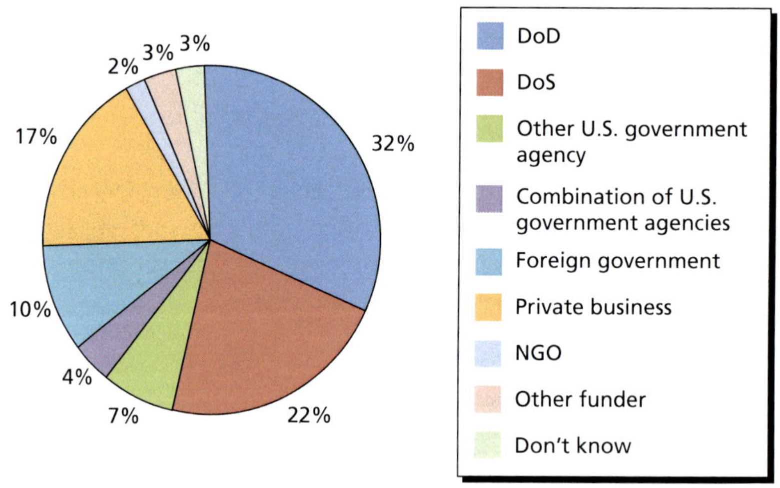

RAND *RR420-1.2*

[3] Despite the common perception that armed contractors are necessarily equivalent to land security contractors (referred to as private security contractors, or PSCs), not all security contractors in our survey sample were armed, and not all respondents who reported carrying a weapon as part of their job were land security contractors. Only 67 percent of those who reported carrying a weapon were land security contractors. Although 89 percent of land security contractors in our sample carried weapons, 44 percent of contractors engaged in other tasks carried them as well.

Figure 1.3
Job Specialty During Most Recent Contract

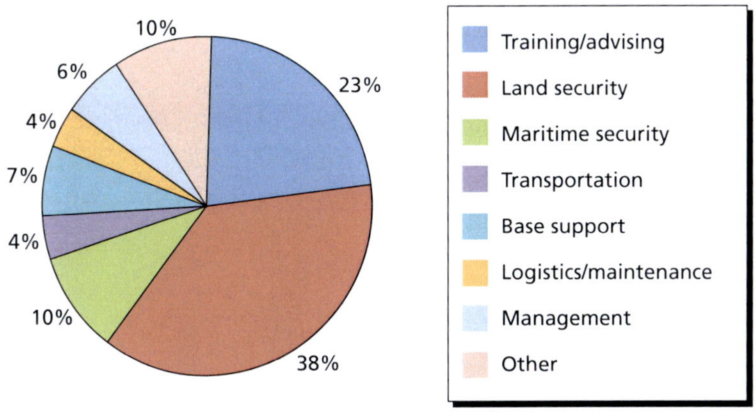

RAND *RR420-1.3*

Figure 1.4
Citizenship of Survey Respondents

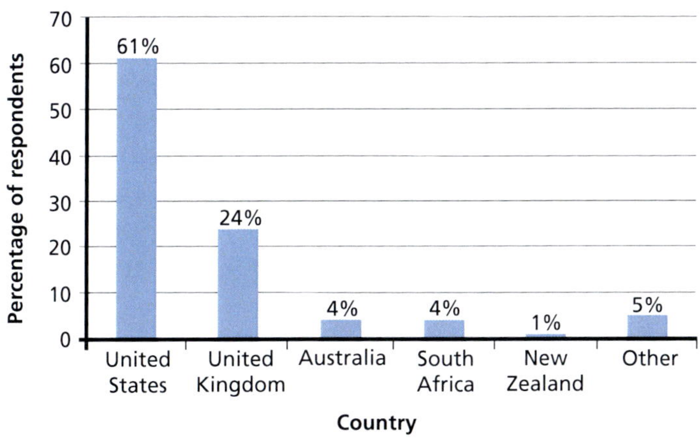

NOTE: "Other" includes Bosnia and Herzegovina, Canada, Chile, Colombia, Croatia, the Czech Republic, Estonia, France, Germany, Greece, India, Italy, Kenya, Lebanon, Macedonia, the Netherlands, the Philippines, Poland, and Romania.

RAND *RR420-1.4*

the sample, citizens of New Zealand accounted for 1 percent, and contractors of other nationalities accounted for 5 percent.

Two-thirds (66 percent) of survey respondents were over the age of 40 (and 32 percent were 50 or older), as shown in Figure 1.5. This is unsurprising, given previous reports and interview evidence that contractors who work in conflict environ-

Figure 1.5
Age of Survey Respondents

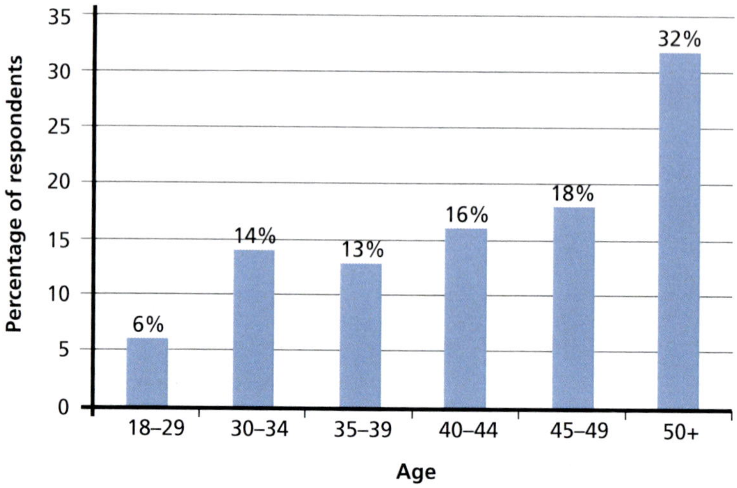

RAND *RR420-1.5*

ments, and particularly PSCs, are often former or retired military personnel (Dunigan, 2011; Spearin, 2006).

On the whole, it appears that the sample of contractors responding to the RAND survey may have a different composition than the general contractor population operating under contract with DoD in fiscal year (FY) 2012. Indeed, the ratio of DoD PSCs to DoD logistics support contractors operating on all DoD contracts in FY 2012 was lower than in our sample (see Table 1.1). However, the ratio of DoD PSCs to DoD training contractors during that time period was higher (DoD, 2012). We therefore recognize that our sample may not be representative of the general contractor population.

Table 1.1
Comparison of RAND Survey with DoD Data on Contractors

Characteristic	RAND Survey	DoD Data
Ratio of DoD PSCs to DoD logistics support contractors (all theaters)	10.5:1	6:1
Ratio of DoD PSCs to DoD training contractors (all theaters)	5:3	2:1

SOURCE: DoD data come from the *FY 2012 DoD Services Contract Inventory* (DoD, 2012).

Organization of This Report

The remainder of this report begins with a review of the relevant government, industry, scholarly, and media literature in Chapter Two. Chapter Three details our findings on the deployment experiences of the contractors surveyed for this project, including an examination of their military history, the number of times they have deployed on contract, the length of their most recent deployment on contract, preparation for deployment on contract, combat exposure while deployed on contract, and living conditions while deployed on contract. Chapter Four describes our findings on the mental health status of the contractors surveyed for this project, including assessments of the prevalence of probable PTSD, depression, high-risk alcohol use, and tobacco use. Chapter Five builds on this analysis to detail our findings on respondents' general health and physical health status. Chapter Six describes our findings on contractors' access to care, with an emphasis on mental health care services. Chapter Seven includes a summary of our findings and our policy recommendations. The report concludes with two appendixes that provide additional data from our analyses in Chapters Three and Four and the results of our imputation analysis, respectively.

CHAPTER TWO

The Health Status of Contractors Who Are Deployed to Conflict Environments Is Not Well Understood: A Review of the Literature

Much has been written on military and security privatization, but very little is known about the experiences of individual contractors deployed to conflict environments. Media coverage and popular writing on contractors tend to focus on three main themes: lack of government oversight, contractor waste and fraud, and regulation of contractors (see, e.g., Pelton, 2007; Scahill, 2007). Academic scholarship on the topic tends to fall into three broad categories: the theoretical implications of outsourcing as an abrogation of state sovereignty, issues of accountability and regulation, and civil-military relations and contractors' effects on the military (Avant, 2005; Chesterman, 2010–2011; Cotton et al., 2010; Dunigan, 2011; Kinsey, 2006; Krahmann, 2010).

Despite the large and growing body of work on military and security privatization, little is known about the psychological and sociological implications of contractors' presence in conflict environments. Specifically, much reporting on the mental health and well-being of contractors during and after deployment has been limited to individual interviews and anecdotal accounts from a handful of contractor staff and their families who are willing to speak about their experiences. These accounts are most commonly found in popular media, such as blogs and websites intended to advocate for individual contractors or to serve as a resource for those facing mental health challenges.[1]

To provide context for the findings from our survey, this chapter describes the existing literature on physical and mental health risks affecting contractors, the reported prevalence of mental health problems among contractors compared with military personnel, initiatives from the contracting industry to address contractors' mental health and well-being, the stigma among the contractor population associated with seeking mental health services, and the role of the DBA in addressing the health needs of contractors who have been injured while employed on contract for the U.S. government.[2]

[1] One example is the website "American Contractors in Iraq" (http://www.americancontractorsiniraq.com).

[2] The Defense Base Act of 1941 requires contracting firms to purchase workers' compensation insurance for employees and subcontractor staff working at overseas military bases and other locations outside the United States. According to a 2009 report by the DoD Inspector General, citing a 2008 memo from the House Committee on Oversight and Government Reform, "for 90 percent of the DBA insurance required in Iraq and Afghani-

Physical and Mental Health Risks Faced by Contractors in Conflict Environments

Contractors operating in a conflict environment have been and continue to be exposed to gunfire, mortar attacks, rocket-propelled grenades, improvised explosive devices (IEDs), and other modes of attack; chemical inhalation from "burn pits";[3] ambushes; kidnappings; exchanges of gunfire with Iraqi or Afghan insurgents; the deaths of fellow contractors, military personnel, and local civilians; dismemberment as the result of IEDs or roadside bombs; the handling or uncovering human remains; and the psychological aftermath of killing.[4] Contractors operating outside of forward operating bases are exposed to particularly high levels of risk, including the risk of death.[5]

In 2010, T. Christian Miller of *ProPublica* was the first to report that contractor deaths had exceeded those among military personnel in Iraq and Afghanistan. According to data from the U.S. Department of Labor and DoD, from January through June 2010, more than 250 civilians died in those conflicts, compared with 235 service members (Miller, 2010b). The two highest-risk contracted jobs are armed security and convoy driving through hostile environments (see, e.g., "Halliburton Hit Hard by Iraq Kidnappings," 2004).[6] Other contractors who face a particularly high level of risk are translators, whose visibility makes them more likely to be held hostage or kidnapped.

Contractors are prohibited by both international law and international and national industry standards from engaging in offensive combat (American National Standards Institute and ASIS International, 2012, p. 36; *Montreux Document*, 2008), but many operate in the same environments and are believed to be exposed to at least the same level of risk as military personnel. Schooner and Swan of George Wash-

---

stan, the premiums and other terms were negotiated between the private contractors and the insurance companies while the costs were paid by the Federal Government. DBA workers' compensation benefits include disability, medical, and death benefits for injury or death in the course of employment. Injured contractor personnel are entitled to receive coverage for medical costs" (DoD, Office of the Inspector General, 2009, p. 3).

[3] Burn pits have been a common method of waste disposal on overseas bases in conflict zones. A 2011, a U.S. Army memorandum outlined the potential long-term health effects of exposure to burn pits for both the service members and contractors at Bagram Air Base in Afghanistan, including "reduced lung function or exacerbated chronic bronchitis, chronic pulmonary disease, asthma, atherosclerosis, or other cardiopulmonary diseases" (Pratt, 2011; see also Drummond, 2012; Zajac, 2013).

[4] One survey of UK-based private contractors working in Iraq identified the following primary stressors: "thought [he or she] might be killed or seriously wounded," "came under small arms fire," "came under enemy sniper fire," "saw UK/allied forces killed or wounded," "discharged weapon at enemy," "encountered hostile or aggressive reactions from civilians," and "handled or uncovered human remains" (Messenger et al., 2012, p. 861).

[5] In one widely reported 2004 incident in Fallujah, Iraq, four contractors providing convoy security were attacked and killed by insurgents, their bodies mutilated, burned, and hung from a bridge (Gettleman, 2004; Kelly, 2011).

[6] As of April 2013 (the most recently available statistics at the time of this writing), it was reported that 259 private contractors had been killed in Iraq and 1,378 had been killed in Afghanistan (Office of the Deputy Assistant Secretary of Defense for Program Support, 2013).

ington University Law School analyzed this risk by comparing uniformed personnel deaths with contractor deaths, concluding that private security contractors working for DoD were 1.8 to 4.5 times more likely to be killed than their military counterparts (Schooner and Swan, 2010).[7]

A 2009 DoD Inspector General report offers some indication of the health risks faced by contractors. The review found that the number of contractors treated at medical treatment facilities (MTFs) in Iraq, Afghanistan, and Kuwait placed a significant burden on MTF staff and that there was no billing or collection process in place to recoup the costs of treating these patients. The MTFs in Baghdad, Iraq, and at Bagram Air Base in Afghanistan treated the largest number of contractors, with Baghdad reporting that contractors accounted for "at least" 33 percent of its outpatient visits (DoD, Office of the Inspector General, 2009, pp. 7–9). Although the numbers cited in the report might indicate that contractors are exposed to a significant amount of risk and require medical care as a result, MTF staff stated that "contractor personnel tended to have more chronic medical conditions," adding that it "became a burden when specialty care had to be arranged" (DoD, Office of the Inspector General, 2009, p. 8).

Despite the U.S. military's acknowledgement of the prevalence of medical challenges facing private contractors, the U.S. government has largely remained silent. In 2008, Congress established the Commission on Wartime Contracting to identify issues of concern regarding contracting in expeditionary operations (see DoD, 2009). The commission's report emphasized eight issues of immediate concern from the U.S. government's perspective. It did not mention contractor training or the need to screen contractor personnel for mental health problems, nor did it address the prevalence of these problems during and after deployment. Like the Commission on Wartime Contracting, the Commission on Army Acquisition and Program Management in Expeditionary Operations, also known as the Gansler Commission, reviewed contracting practices in the context of civilian-military cooperation but did not address the health or well-being of contractors (Commission on Army Acquisition and Program Management in Expeditionary Operations, 2007).

The risks to contractors' physical health are intertwined with risks to their mental health. As Messenger et al. (2012, p. 856) explain, PTSD is "characterized by feelings of intense fear, helplessness, or horror and symptoms of reexperiencing, avoidance and hyperarousal," pointing to the perceived "significant threat to life associated with private security work, a factor widely accepted to be one of the best predictors of PTSD" (p. 866). In a 2007 article on private contractors, the *Christian Science Monitor* acknowledged the prevalence of deployment-related physical and mental health challenges among members of the contractor community and stated that "an unknown number experience symptoms of PTSD" (Knickerbocker, 2007).

---

[7] According to Miller (2009c), "The Houston engineering and construction firm [KBR] reported more than 700 serious injuries or deaths in the first six months of 2007—almost five incidents for every 100 workers."

One of the prevailing themes in coverage of the physical and mental health risks to deployed contractors is a perceived lack of support both during and after deployment. For example, Messenger et al. (2012) cite a lack of operational support (i.e., backup) and situational control as significant factors linking "subjective appraisals of trauma" and PTSD. In addition, sociological factors, such as "mistrust between teammates" (particularly among local national contractors), a "perceived lack of employer organized support," and ambiguities related to employment status at the end of a deployment could—they argue—"indicate an increased risk for mental health difficulties" (Messenger et al., 2012, p. 864).

Prevalence of Mental Health Problems Among Contractors Compared with Military Personnel

Given the various health risks facing contractors, what do the available data tell us about the existence of mental health problems among this population? Statistics on mental health problems, such as PTSD, among U.S. military personnel are widely available and have been a topic of study since the early years of the conflicts in Iraq and Afghanistan. A 2006 study by Hoge, Auchterlonie, and Milliken found differences in the prevalence of mental health problems between U.S. soldiers and marines deployed to Iraq (with 19.1 percent screening positive for PTSD, major depression, or other mental health problems) and those deployed to Afghanistan (11.3 percent). This is believed to be because personnel deployed to Iraq experienced a sustained higher level of combat exposure than those deployed to Afghanistan (Hoge and Castro, 2005, pp.11-2–11-3). It is unclear whether these and other findings are applicable to contractors serving in these same environments, however.

More recently, the Institute of Medicine reported that 44 percent of U.S. troops deployed to Iraq or Afghanistan experienced mental health problems upon their return (Institute of Medicine, 2013). According to that report, "in the scientific literature, the estimates of prevalence of those service members who served in the two conflicts range from 4 to 20 percent for PTSD, 5 to 37 percent for depression, and 4.7 to 39 percent for problematic alcohol abuse" (Institute of Medicine, 2013).

The prevalence of mental health problems also appears to vary across coalition troops from different countries, with lower rates among UK troops than among U.S. troops (Sundin et al., 2010). UK studies have found stronger associations between combat and alcohol misuse than between combat and PTSD or other common mental health disorders (Browne et al., 2008; Fear et al., 2010). The reasons for these cross-national differences, which may also be reflected in cross-national contractor samples, are unclear. Differences might arise from a wide variety of factors, including differences in vulnerability, sample selection, military culture, cohesion within operational units, psychological treatment, disability policies, or different levels of exposure to traumatic events and attendant responses.

However, there is little or no data on the prevalence of mental health problems among contractors who work in conflict environments. Neil Greenberg, a psychiatrist, PTSD expert, and co-author of the aforementioned Messenger et al. study, summarized the state of the field in 2012:

> Over the past 15 years there has been extensive research into the mental health of military personnel, but we know very little about the mental health of security contractors. Security contractors have often worked in the Armed Forces and are likely to have experienced many traumatic events whilst still in service. Quite how they might have been affected by the military service or indeed by their work in the security industry is currently unknown. (Greenberg, 2012)

Just two academic studies have examined the health and well-being of contractors. The first (Feinstein and Botes, 2009) involved administering a web-based psychiatric test to 79 deployed and recently returned contractors, collecting data on three topics: demographics, trauma history, and the severity of depression or other psychological distress. Twenty percent of the survey population scored above the cutoff point for clinically significant depression, and the study found significant correlations between PTSD symptoms and depression and between depression and exposure to lifetime trauma. Demographic data showed that the contractors—all male and with a median age of 43 years old (approximately 15 years older than the average U.S. soldier)—had been working in conflict zones for an average of 3.5 years and spent an average of 7.5 months per year away from home. Despite the small study sample, conclusions from these preliminary data suggest that a significant minority of contractors working in conflict zones, particularly Iraq, have experienced psychological problems (Feinstein and Botes, 2009).

The second academic study of the effects of contractor deployment (Messenger et al., 2012) focused on the experiences of security contractors working in Iraq. In this qualitative study of seven contractors, Messenger et al. sought to collect individual perceptions of occupational experience, drawing inferences about the conflict environment, level of risk, and mental health issues. The results confirmed that contractors are exposed to the same stressors known to increase the risk of psychiatric problems among military personnel. For example, participants experienced "multiple episodes of potentially traumatic events, such as coming under small arms, artillery and rocket fire; having a friend injured or killed nearby; and having an IED explode nearby" (Messenger et al., 2012, p. 860). Contractors also reported unique stressors, including an absence of backup in private security combat situations, difficulty forming trusting relationships (particularly among local national contractors), a perceived lack of employer-organized support, and ambiguity in their employment status at the end of the contract. Messenger et al. (2012, p. 864) point to all of these factors as potential contributors to mental health challenges for contractors. Critically, contractors also cited the stigma associated with psychological treatment as a deterrent to seeking help in coping with the effects of their deployment experiences, as discussed later in this chapter. Although the study did not provide concrete data on the prevalence of PTSD among deployed contractors, its findings contribute to the small body of evidence on contractors' exposure to environments that have been shown to correlate with mental health problems among military personnel.

The international literature on the effects of deployment on contractors is equally scarce. In 2008, the Geneva Centre for the Democratic Control of Armed Forces, in collaboration with the United Nations and the Organization for Security and Co-operation in Europe, released the *Gender and Security Sector Reform Toolkit* to encourage a higher level of gender awareness and integration in security-sector reform policies and programming. The toolkit includes a section on the mental and physical health of contracted employees in "high-risk, high-stress conflict areas such as Afghanistan and Iraq." Although the authors confirm that it is a "little researched area," the available research suggests that, "contractors suffer the same kinds of combat-related mental health problems that affect returning military personnel" (Schulz and Yeung, 2008, p. 8; see also Risen, 2007).

Industry-Led Mental Health and Well-Being Initiatives

The lack of empirical research on the health status of contractor personnel does not mean that the contracting industry has not taken steps to address the problems outlined here. Several companies have issued publications acknowledging employees' potential exposure to physical and mental health risks while deployed. For example, a 2012 pamphlet from the Security Association for the Maritime Industry, "Psychological Support for Private Maritime Security Companies," offers advice for companies in addressing mental health challenges among their employees. However, it also states that the majority of contractor personnel come to the profession with prior military experience, adding, "During their military service they are likely to have encountered a wide range of stressful experiences and hopefully they will have dealt successfully with the challenges which military life throws up from time to time" (Security Association for the Maritime Industry, 2012).

Individual private companies have also developed programs to address the psychological challenges facing contractors, though there is limited publicly available information on how these programs are structured or the types of support they offer. For example, Mission Critical Psychological Services is a U.S.-based firm that provides psychological support services to firms in the contracting industry. Asked to estimate the number of contractors suffering from mental health issues, its CEO stated, "I think the numbers are in the thousands, maybe tens of thousands. Many are going undiagnosed. These guys are fighting demons, and they don't know how to cope" (Risen, 2007).[8]

The extent to which the diverse array of contracting companies rely on private providers of psychological services tailored to the industry is unclear. However, recent U.S. and international codes and standards aimed at regulating the private *security* industry, in particular, clearly mandate that these firms establish policies that promote a safe and healthy working environment, including policies that address the psychological health of employees. One such requirement is embedded in the American National Standards Institute/ASIS International document *Management System for Quality of Private Security Company Operations* (known as the PSC.1 standard), which states, "The organization shall establish, implement, and maintain procedures to promote a safe and healthy working environment including reasonable precautions to protect people working on its behalf in high-risk or life threatening operations consistent with legal, regulatory, and contractual obligations." One of the procedures specified is "medical and psychological health awareness training, care, and support" (American National Standards Institute and ASIS International, 2012, p. 24). The inclusion of such a requirement in the PSC.1 standard is significant, because compliance with the standard is now mandated in all DoD- and UK government–funded contracts. Moreover, the International Code of Conduct, a multi-stakeholder initiative aimed at industry self-regulation to which more than 600 private security companies are now signatories, includes a similar provision requiring that signatory companies adopt policies that support a safe and healthy working environment. This requirement specifically mentions a requirement for policies that address psychological health ("International Code of Conduct for Private Security Service Providers," 2010, section 64d, p. 14).

Because these are relatively new industry standards, company measures to address these requirements are still evolving. For the time being, it appears that a number of firms rely on traditional corporate employee assistance programs to provide the required psychological support for their personnel,[9] but consulting firms, such as Mission Critical Psychological Services in the United States or March on Stress in the United Kingdom, could likely be used to fulfill the requirements as well.[10] While

---

[8] The CEO of Mission Critical Psychological Services, Paul Brand, was formerly a senior vice president at DynCorp International, and his firm now provides services to DynCorp. Brand told the *New York Times* in 2007 that "twenty-four percent of the DynCorp police trainers [providing training to Iraqi police personnel on behalf of the U.S. Department of State] showed symptoms of post-traumatic stress disorder after their deployment." According to the article, "[Brand] and others said they knew of no other studies that formally assessed the problem among private workers in Iraq" (Risen, 2007).

[9] Personal communication with a private security industry expert, 2013.

[10] According to its website, Mission Critical Psychological Services is a U.S.-based consulting firm that works with companies to "screen applicants for psychological fitness; provide training, counseling, and support during missions; and debrief upon return." Similarly, March on Stress is a UK-based psychological health consultancy

the effectiveness of employee assistance programs in addressing the mental health needs of this population fell outside the scope of this study, it presents an interesting question for future research.

Stigma in Seeking Professional Mental Health Care

The dearth of empirical research on the physical and psychological well-being of contractors stands in sharp contrast to the websites, blogs, articles, and autobiographical accounts by and about individual private contractors (see, e.g., Geraghty, 2008; Clark, 2012; Fainaru, 2008; Phinney, 2005; Kelly, 2011). The website of the advocacy group American Contractors in Iraq offers a host of information about PTSD and accessing treatment, crisis referral services, and local support groups ("American Contractors in Iraq," undated). Despite the wealth of informal sources of information on the topic, help-seeking for mental health challenges remains heavily stigmatized in the contractor community. Geographical and socioeconomic barriers may further complicate efforts to access professional services. According to DBA plaintiffs' attorney Gary Pitts, in the United States, "many contractors live in small towns or rural areas without access to high-quality mental health workers" (Risen, 2007).

In their study, Messenger et al. found that "most participants were resistant to seeking help for psychological distress and tended to view a career in private security as incompatible with seeking help for psychiatric difficulties" (Messenger et al., 2012, p. 864). These conclusions mirror those of studies examining the well-being of deployed military personnel. For example, in a review of findings from the Walter Reed Army Institute of Research Land Combat Study, Hoge and Castro state that "soldiers and Marines are not very likely to seek professional help if they have a mental health problem" because of the perceived stigma of doing so (Hoge and Castro, 2005, p. 11-3).

Research has shown that stigma can serve as a barrier to receiving mental health treatment among both UK and U.S. service members (see Table 2.1). In both countries' militaries, service members with a mental health diagnosis or who screen positive for a mental health disorder express greater concern about stigma than those without a diagnosis or who do not screen positive (Hoge et al., 2004; Iversen et al., 2009). Generally, a higher percentage of UK service members expressed agreement with statements about stigma-related barriers to care than did U.S. service members. Among UK service members, the greatest concerns were about being treated differently by unit leaders and about peers having less confidence in them. Among U.S. service members, the greatest concern was being seen as weak.

---

that helps "build resilience by safeguarding the psychological wellbeing of those personnel through the prevention, detection and treatment of occupational and operational stress."

Table 2.1
Comparing the Beliefs of U.S. and UK Service Members with and Without Mental Health Diagnoses or Positive Screenings for Mental Health Disorders

	UK Military		U.S. Military	
% of service members agreeing with the following statement	Respondents Without a Diagnosis or Positive Screening	Respondents with a Diagnosis or Positive Screening	Respondents Without a Diagnosis or Positive Screening	Respondents with a Diagnosis or Positive Screening
It would be too embarrassing.	33.6	40.6–70.5	13.3–13.5	24.0–28.6
It would harm my career.	45.3	50.8–57.5	12.6–15.4	27.5–29.2
Members of my unit might have less confidence in me.	71.9	68.5–83.5	21.1–23.9	33.3–41.6
My unit bosses/leaders might treat me differently.	69.7	76.1–83.5	21.1–23.7	30.9–46.0
My bosses/leaders would blame me for the problem.	11.2	24.9–45.7	13.0–13.4	19.7–33.9
I would be seen as weak by those who are important to me.	36.1	51.7–57.6	22.8–25.8	29.5–48.9

SOURCES: Gould, Adler, et al., 2010; Iversen et al., 2011; Joint Mental Health Advisory Team 7, 2011.

The correlation between seeking treatment for mental health concerns and perceptions of weakness, untrustworthiness, and being unfit to work has been reported among contractors as well (Messenger et al., 2012). Messenger et al. cite cultural factors common to the military and deployed contractors as possible contributors to these perceptions: "It is likely that factors believed to amplify resistance to seeking help among military personnel, such as the culture of resilience, courage, and masculine stereotypes, are also likely to be relevant for those working in private security" (Messenger et al., 2012, p. 865).

However, it is important to note that surveys find that the general civilian population is also fearful of negative outcomes as a result of seeking treatment (Jorm, 2000; Mojtabai, 2007; Substance Abuse and Mental Health Services Administration, 2012). Among the general U.S. population, 36 percent said that they would feel embarrassed or very embarrassed if their friends knew that they were getting professional help (Mojtabai, 2007). In a 2010 U.S. study, 10 percent of respondents reported not seeking mental health treatment because other members of the community or neighbors could have a negative opinion, and the same proportion did not want others to find out about their treatment-seeking. In the same study, 8 percent of respondents indicated that they feared that there would be negative repercussions for their job (Substance Abuse and Mental Health Services Administration, 2012). In the United

Kingdom, there have been numerous nationwide anti-stigma social marketing campaigns to address concerns surrounding this stigma (see, for example, Evans-Lacko, Henderson, and Thornicroft, 2013).

Denial of Defense Base Act Claims

The DBA mandates that all contractors working overseas under a U.S. government–funded contract (e.g., contracts funded by DoD, DoS, the U.S. Agency for International Development, and others) have access to workers' compensation insurance. The DBA requires contracting firms to obtain workers' compensation insurance coverage for injuries and deaths sustained as a result of work on U.S. government contracts that is performed outside the United States. Taxpayers pay the premiums, which are built into contract costs, and the government reimburses insurance carriers for combat-related injuries and deaths (Office of the Under Secretary of Defense for Acquisition, Technology, and Logistics, 2009; Miller, 2009a).

In a series of articles for *ProPublica*, T. Christian Miller reported on the types of physical and mental health problems affecting contractors, including loss of limbs, burns, loss of hearing or eyesight, various wounds (such as from shrapnel, gunshots, mortar attacks, or IEDs), PTSD, TBI, depression, suicidal ideation, and suicide. Despite the reported frequency and severity of these problems, Miller (2009a) found that between 2002 and 2007, "insurers had denied 44 percent of all serious injury claims" under the DBA and that they "also turned down 60 percent of contractors who claimed to suffer psychological damage, such as post-traumatic stress disorder." He highlights systemic flaws in the DBA—along with a lack of regulation and enforcement by the U.S. Department of Labor and the monopoly of insurance company AIG—as contributors to the high rate of DBA claim denial.[11]

The *ProPublica* investigation led Congress to launch an inquiry into how claims are handled by both the U.S. Department of Labor and AIG. It concluded that the DBA is deeply flawed and acknowledged the thousands of contractors who have not received help for physical and mental health problems as a result of systemic failures (Miller, 2009b).

---

[11] ProPublica reports that several U.S.-based companies allegedly sent employees abroad under federal contracts without the mandatory workers' compensation insurance (Miller and Smith, 2009). The U.S. Department of Labor and the U.S. Department of Justice declined to pursue charges in any of these cases. Miller's investigation also highlights the monopoly of insurance giant AIG and explores allegations that the company set unprecedented and uncontested high premiums (particularly during the early years of the wars in Iraq and Afghanistan) and was allowed to operate outside of both government regulations and the competitive insurance market. Records indicate that AIG processed 90 percent of all contractor injury claims in Iraq and Afghanistan in 2007 (Miller and Smith, 2009). Of the medical claims filed by contractors, records show that AIG routinely denied two types: those for psychological counseling and those for prosthetic legs (Miller, 2009b; Miller and Smith, 2009).

Conclusion

Despite the paucity of empirical research on the health and well-being of private contractors, there is ample evidence to support the argument that contractors deployed to conflict zones face mental health and physical challenges that are similar to those of their military counterparts, with whom they often work side by side. The number of DBA claims filed, the extent to which contractors make use of MTFs, and data from two small-scale academic studies provide the best-available gauge of the prevalence of these problems among the contractor population. Given that there has been so little empirical research on the health and well-being of contractors working in conflict environments, however, the goal of our study was to explore these issues objectively and more comprehensively than has been done to date, in an effort to provide empirical data and evidence to inform discussion of these issues.

CHAPTER THREE

What Are the Deployment Experiences of Contractors?

As discussed in Chapter Two, deployment experiences likely to play a role in shaping the health and well-being of contractors. Combat exposure, for instance, has been linked to PTSD, depression, and physical health problems in research on the health of U.S. military personnel (Hoge, Auchterlonie, and Milliken, 2006; Seal et al., 2009). Again, due to the fact that contractors are deployed to theaters of conflict alongside military forces, it is reasonable to examine the extent to which these variables play a role in contractor health and well-being.

It was crucial to gain a more solid understanding of how contractors in our sample experienced deployment prior to embarking on an analysis of their health and well-being. To that end, as discussed in Chapter One, our survey included a number of questions on contractors' perceptions of preparedness for deployment, their combat exposure while deployed on contract, and their living conditions while deployed on contract. In addition, the survey ask whether or not they had prior military experience, the number of times they had deployed on contract, and the length of their most recent deployment on contract. In the remainder of this chapter, we present the findings pertaining to these questions and explore variations in deployment preparation, combat exposure, and living conditions by contractor specialty (i.e., job type), contract funder, citizenship, age, whether the respondent carried a weapon as part of his or her job, prior military experience, length of most recent contract, and number of deployments on contract.

Overall Contractor Deployment Experiences

The vast majority (84 percent) of contractors in our sample had previously served in the armed forces, with 14 percent of this subset serving in a military other than that of the United States. This is not surprising, given that prior military experience is a prerequisite for employment for many contracting positions. Many of these personnel were armed as well, with 67 percent of respondents carrying a weapon as part of their job during their most recent deployment on contract.

Meanwhile, contractors in our sample tended to deploy frequently for relatively short periods (see Figures 3.1 and 3.2). Indeed, 65 percent had deployed three or more times on contract, and nearly 50 percent of respondents deployed for six months or less on their most recent contract, compared with 21 percent deploying for seven months or longer. Approximately one-third (33 percent) of the sample was deployed at the time of the survey.

Figure 3.1
Number of Deployments on Contract

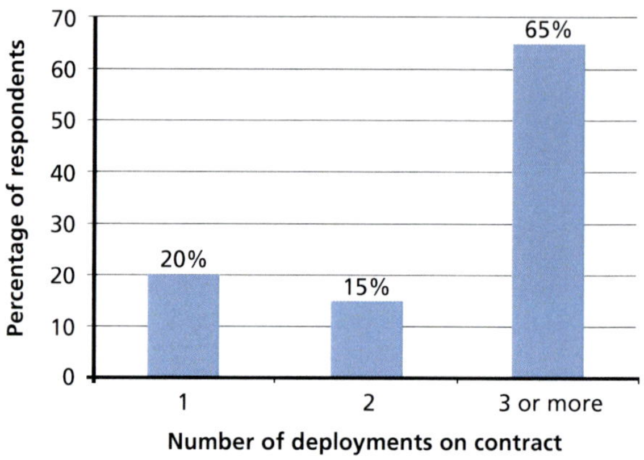

RAND *RR420-3.1*

Figure 3.2
Length of Most Recent Deployment on Contract

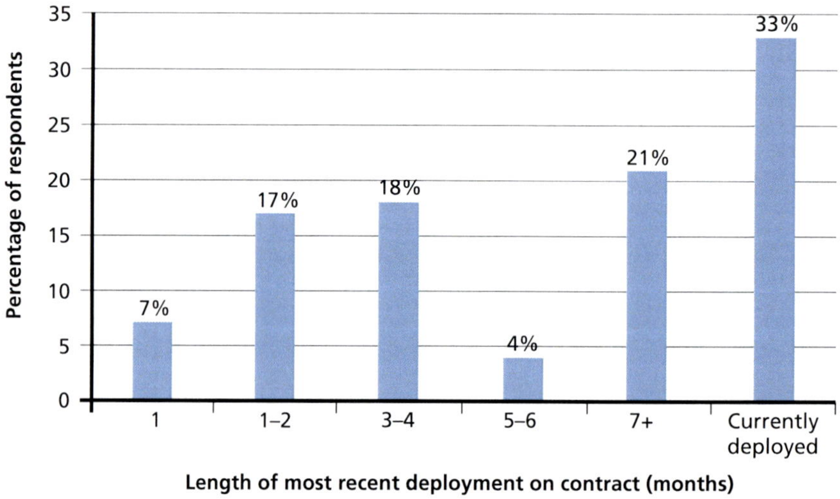

RAND *RR420-3.2*

As discussed in Chapter One, we assessed respondents' perceived preparation for deployment, combat exposure, and living conditions using modified scales from the DRRI. On these scales, higher scores indicate better preparation for deployment, more combat exposure, and better living conditions, respectively. Table 3.1 presents the mean scores for the entire sample on each of these scales, illustrating that, on the whole, contractors in the sample felt somewhat prepared for their deployment (mean = 7.06 on a scale of 0–12), experienced fairly low levels of combat exposure (mean = 4.92 on a scale of 0–24), and had moderately comfortable living conditions while deployed on contract (mean = 12.13 on a scale of 0–17).

When examining deployment experiences while controlling for contractors' job specialty, contract funder, citizenship, age, whether they carried a weapon as part of their job, prior military experience, length of most recent contract, and number of deployments on contract, several interesting distinctions emerge. These bivariate analyses are discussed in greater detail in the following sections with respect to deployment preparation, combat exposure, and living conditions, respectively.

Table 3.1
Contractor Deployment Experiences, Overall

Characteristic	Number	Mean (std)/%
DRRI: perception of preparation for deployment (higher score = more prepared, range 0–12)	580	7.06 (3.43)
DRRI: combat exposure (higher score = more exposure, range 0–24)	559	4.92 (5.52)
DRRI: living conditions (higher score = better living conditions, range 0–17)	539	12.13 (3.32)
Carried a weapon as part of job	606	66.5%
Prior military experience	646	83.9%
Length of most recent deployment	617	
Less than 2 months	152	24.6%
3–6 months	143	23.2%
7+ months	126	20.4%
Currently deployed	196	31.8%
Number of deployments on contract with company	617	
1	123	19.9%
2	93	15.1%
3 or more	401	65.0%

Predeployment Training and Preparation

The data presented in Table 3.1 indicate that, on the whole, contractors reported feeling fairly well prepared for their deployments, but an exploration of responses to the individual items on the modified DRRI scale provides interesting insight into the distinct areas in which contractors felt most and least prepared. While a majority of contractors reported feeling prepared for the operational aspects of deployment—that is, they felt that they had received adequate training, administrative and logistical support, intelligence, and so on—only approximately one-quarter of respondents reported having access to adequate resources to deal with stress, and slightly less than that reported that their company had provided them with adequate stress management training (see Table 3.2).

Next, we turn to the bivariate analyses mentioned earlier, looking first at distinctions in deployment preparation among contractors with different job specialties (see Table A.1 in Appendix A). Contractors involved in logistics and maintenance tasks reported being the best prepared for deployment of all contracting job special-

Table 3.2
Individual DRRI Deployment Preparation Items

DRRI Preparation Items	% in Agreement
I was informed about the role my unit was expected to play in the deployment. (n = 572)	76.9
When I was deployed I had a pretty good idea of how long the mission would take to complete. (n = 571)	76.5
I was adequately trained to work the shifts required of me during my deployment. (n = 572)	71.3
The equipment I was given functioned the way it was supposed to. (n = 577)	70.4
I received adequate training on how to use my equipment. (n = 573)	68.0
I had all the supplies and equipment needed to get my job done. (n = 580)	66.6
When I was deployed I felt I had adequate administrative/logistical support for travel and mission requirements. (n = 574)	61.7
I was accurately informed of what daily life would be like during my deployment. (n = 573)	61.3
When I was deployed I felt that I had been prepared with adequate, accurate intelligence to support my mission. (n = 573)	54.3
I saw as much combat as I expected. (n = 570)	50.5
When I was deployed I had access to adequate resources to help with stress. (n = 574)	25.6
My contracting company provided me with adequate stress management training. (n = 573)	23.6

ties (mean score = 8.17 on a scale of 0–12), while transportation contractors were least prepared (mean score = 5.45 on a scale of 0–12). Base support contractors also reported being relatively poorly prepared for deployment, while management and land security (i.e., contractors not involved in maritime security) were both fairly well prepared, on average. These differences are statistically significant ($p < 0.05$). The findings make sense in light of the fact that transportation and base support positions do not typically require prior military experience as a prerequisite for employment, while land security positions do.

Meanwhile, contractors operating on DoD-funded contracts reported being relatively well prepared for deployment, but their responses are not significantly different from those working on DoS contracts (mean scores = 6.82 versus 6.63, respectively).

Contractors who were UK citizens reported being better prepared for deployment (mean score = 7.24) than those who were U.S. citizens (mean score = 6.66), while contractors hailing from other countries reported being better prepared than either U.S. or UK contractors, on average (mean score = 8.37). These differences are statistically significant ($p < 0.001$). Moreover, contractors carrying a weapon reported being slightly better prepared (mean score = 7.29) than those who did not carry a weapon (mean score = 6.55; $p < 0.05$). The length of respondents' most recent deployment and their number of deployments on contract do not show much variation in terms of reported levels of preparedness for deployment, although it does appear that shorter and more frequent deployments are correlated with higher reported levels of preparedness (see Table A.1 in Appendix A). This finding indicates that feelings of preparedness may grow with repeated deployment experience but that deployment fatigue associated with lengthy deployments may decrease how prepared one feels.

Contractors' Combat Exposure

When examining responses to the individual combat exposure items, one item clearly stands out: Seventy-three percent of respondents reported that they or members of their team were exposed to hostile incoming fire from small arms, artillery, rockets, mortars, or bombs. By contrast, under 40 percent of respondents had encountered land or water mines or booby traps, been in a vehicle that was under fire, been part of a team that suffered casualties, or personally witnessed someone from their team or an ally unit being seriously wounded or killed, and 48 percent reported that they or a member of their team had been attacked by terrorists or civilians (see Table 3.3).

Meanwhile, an examination of respondents' combat exposure across job specialties shows some interesting distinctions (all differences are statistically significant at $p < 0.001$), with contractors providing transportation services reporting significantly higher levels of combat exposure than any other contractors (mean score = 8.78 on a scale of 0–24). In contrast, logistics/maintenance contractors and maritime security

Table 3.3
Individual DRRI Combat Exposure Items

DRRI Combat Exposure Items	% of Respondents with Any Exposure
I or members of my team encountered land or water mines and/or booby traps. (n = 553)	36.2
I or members of my team received hostile incoming fire from small arms, artillery, rockets, mortars, or bombs. (n = 554)	72.7
I was in a vehicle (for example, a truck, tank, armored personnel carrier, helicopter, plane, or boat) that was under fire. (n = 548)	39.4
I or members of my team were attacked by terrorists or civilians. (n = 553)	47.4
My team suffered casualties. (n = 549)	34.1
I personally witnessed someone from my team or an ally unit being seriously wounded or killed. (n = 554)	36.3

contractors both reported very low levels of combat exposure (mean score = 3.02 and 3.05, respectively), and base support contractors reported fairly low levels as well (mean score = 4.27). None of the other specialties approached the level of combat exposure reported by transportation contractors, with training/advising contractors reporting the second-highest level of combat exposure at several points below that reported by transportation contractors (mean score = 5.41). These findings are relatively unsurprising, given the nature of the most recent conflicts to which contractors have been deployed in large numbers: It makes sense that contractors who have to travel "outside the wire" in transport convoys (i.e., transportation contractors) would be more likely to have encountered conflict situations, particularly IEDs, while those operating primarily on bases (i.e., logistics/maintenance or base support contractors) or at sea (i.e., maritime security contractors) would be less likely to have come into frequent contact with combat situations.[1]

Also interesting is the fact that U.S. contractors reported significantly higher levels of combat exposure than either UK contractors or those who were citizens of other countries (mean score = 5.52, versus 3.90 and 3.80, respectively, $p < 0.05$). This is in line with a clear trend in the survey data distinguishing between the experiences and health and well-being of U.S. and UK contractors, as explored later in this report. Finally, longer deployments are correlated with higher levels of combat exposure to a statistically significant degree. Table A.2 in Appendix A presents the bivariate analyses, including significance tests, for combat exposure.

---

[1] We should note, however, that maritime security personnel are typically deployed specifically for counterpiracy operations, often in high-threat areas. While they may report less *frequent* combat exposure than their land security counterparts, we do recognize the inherent dangers in counterpiracy missions and in maritime security contracting to support these efforts.

Contractors' Living Conditions

Examining the individual items on the DRRI living conditions scale is slightly more complex than examining the items on the previous two scales, because slightly fewer than half of the items on this scale must be reverse-coded. Table 3.4 presents the positively coded items from our modified living conditions scale, in which higher scores indicate better living conditions, and Table 3.5 shows these reverse-coded items, for which higher scores indicate worse living conditions. For the items in both tables, a score of 1 indicates "almost none of the time," while a score of 5 indicates "almost all of the time." In other words, higher scores indicate items that were more frequently reported. Analysis of the mean scores, shown in both tables, revealed that the most significant complaints were a failure to receive mail in a timely manner, being subjected to loud noises, and long workdays. On the other hand, respondents reported that, most of the time, they had access to clean clothing when they needed it, they could get a cold drink when they wanted one, and they had access to bathrooms or showers when they needed them. Moreover, respondents reported that only a few times, on average, did they have very poor quality food to eat, live in extremely unsanitary conditions, or feel pressure to conform to the local culture to an extent that made it difficult for them to do their job. Overall, it is worth noting that there were no positively coded mean scores below 3, and there was only one reverse-coded mean score above a 3, indicating that, on average, the contractors surveyed experienced fairly comfortable living conditions during their deployments.

Table 3.4
Individual DRRI Living Conditions Items, Positively Coded

DRRI Living Conditions (+)	Mean Score
I had access to clean clothing when I needed it (n = 539)	4.5
I could get a cold drink (for example, water, juice, etc.) when I wanted one. (n = 536)	4.4
I had access to bathrooms or showers when I needed them. (n = 538)	4.3
I got as much sleep as I needed. (n = 539)	3.4
I was able to get enough privacy. (n = 539)	3.4
I got the R&R (rest and relaxation) that I needed. (n = 535)	3.4
I got my mail in a timely manner. (n = 531)	3.1
I had access to phone/internet for managing personal business (for example, to pay bills) and for maintaining contact with family/friends. (n = 538)	3.9
I had the equipment or supplies to do what I needed to do. (n = 530)	3.8
I felt comfortable living in the culture or cultures where I was deployed. (n = 538)	3.8

Table 3.5
Individual DRRI Living Conditions Items, Reverse-Coded

DRRI Living Conditions (–)	Mean
The food I had to eat was of very poor quality (for example, bad or old MREs). (n = 539)	2.1
The conditions I lived in were extremely unsanitary. (n = 537)	2.0
The living space was too crowded. (n = 537)	2.6
The workdays were too long. (n = 537)	2.9
I was subjected to loud noises. (n = 537)	3.3
My daily activities were restricted because of local religious or ethnic customs. (n = 536)	2.4
I felt pressure to conform to the local culture, making it difficult for me to do my job. (n = 538)	1.9

Our exploration of contractors' reported living conditions across job specialties did not turn up any statistically significant differences. However, given the analyses of deployment preparation and combat exposure by job specialty, it is worth noting that transportation contractors reported the worst living conditions of all job specialties (mean score = 10.36 on a scale of 0–17), and maritime security and logistics/maintenance contractors reported the most comfortable living conditions (mean scores of 12.95 and 12.52, respectively). Meanwhile, contractors working on both DoD- and DoS-funded contracts reported equivalent levels of comfort in their living conditions, while contractors working on contracts funded by other entities reported slightly more comfortable living conditions.

Differences in reported living conditions by citizenship were more drastic, with U.S. contractors reporting significantly worse living conditions (mean score = 11.6) than their counterparts hailing from the United Kingdom (mean score = 12.9) or other countries (mean score = 13.3). (These differences are statistically significant at $p < 0.001$.) The reason for these differences is not immediately clear; it may be due to differences in the types of jobs performed by contractors of different nationalities (i.e., more dangerous jobs may correlate with sparser living conditions), differences in the clients or companies that tend to contract with these respective contractors (and the living conditions that they offer on their contracts), or differences in the areas of operation where contractors are operating. Alternatively, differences in reported living conditions may simply reflect divergent expectations among citizens of different countries.

Differences in reported living conditions by length of most recent deployment were also statistically significant ($p < 0.001$), though a clear pattern is difficult to detect. On the whole, deployments lasting less than two months correlated with the best living conditions (mean score = 13.1), while deployments lasting more than seven months correlated with less comfortable living conditions. Table A.3 in Appendix A provides additional detail on the bivariate analyses pertaining to living conditions.

Comparing Contractor and U.S. Military Deployment Experiences

Anecdotal evidence in the literature on contractors who work in conflict environments indicates that, at least as perceived by U.S. troops, contractors tend to deploy with more comfortable living conditions than do U.S. or coalition forces (Dunigan, 2011). However, media reports and at least one lawsuit filed against a private security firm have claimed that contractors are less prepared for deployment on contract than are their military counterparts (*Nordan v. Blackwater Security Consulting, LLC*, 2005; Dalesto, 2012; Peralta, 2012).

In comparing this study's findings on contractor deployment experiences with comparable military survey data reported in King et al. (2006), Vogt et al. (2008), Renshaw (2010), and Chapman et al. (2012)—all of which utilize the DRRI scales to assess U.S. military deployment preparation and living conditions among various military populations—we found that the mean DRRI scores on deployment preparation among all contractors in the RAND sample were very similar to those in the first three military samples.[2] While respondents in the RAND survey reported feeling slightly better prepared than the OIF veterans engaged in service-support activities surveyed by Vogt et al. (statistically significant at $p < 0.05$), they reported feeling virtually the same level of preparation for deployment as the Gulf War veterans surveyed by King et al., the OIF combat and combat support veterans surveyed by Vogt et al., and the National Guard and reserve members surveyed by Renshaw (see Table 3.6).

However, RAND survey respondents reported significantly better living conditions than the Gulf War veterans surveyed by King et al. (2006), as shown in Table 3.6. Although Vogt et al. (2008), Renshaw (2010), and Chapman et al. (2012) did not explore living conditions, the degree of difference between contractor perceptions of living conditions on the RAND survey and the living conditions reported by

---

2 King et al. (2006) were the first to construct the DRRI measures, in an effort to develop an inventory to assess key psychosocial risk and resilience factors for military personnel and veterans deployed to war zones or other hazardous environments. They relied on three U.S. national samples of Gulf War veterans as their evidentiary base in developing the DRRI. Vogt et al.'s (2008) article built on that research to validate the DRRI scales and used a large sample of U.S. Army OIF veterans. Renshaw (2010) used the DRRI measures to assess experiences and postdeployment PTSD symptoms in a sample of 189 Utah National Guard and reserve service members (88 percent Army and 12 percent Air Force) who had served in OEF or OIF (or both). Chapman et al. (2012), meanwhile, examined the deployment preparation, training, and combat experiences of 347 U.S. Army combat medics assigned to line units in OIF or OEF. To make more direct comparisons with the other samples, we took the average of scores on each of the items in the scale and multiplied that average by the number of items used in the scales by King et al. (2006). Possible scores on the DRRI preparedness scale ranged from 14 to 70, and possible scores on the DRRI living conditions scale ranged from 20 to 100.

Table 3.6
Comparing the RAND Contractor Survey to Military Samples: Deployment Preparation and Living Conditions

Sample	Mean (std) DRRI Preparation Items (higher score = more prepared)	Mean (std) DRRI Living Conditions Items (higher score = better living conditions)
RAND contractor survey (all contractors)	49.20 (12.08) n = 580	73.84 (12.63) n = 539
RAND contractor survey (PSCs only)	49.38 (11.66) n = 294	73.81 (13.07) n = 273
Gulf War veterans (n = 357)	48.66 (9.93)	58.15 (13.75)[a]
OIF veterans: combat/combat support (n = 402)	49.84 (10.04)	—
OIF veterans: service-support (n = 238)	47.11 (10.20)[a]	—
OIF and OEF National Guard/reserve service members (n = 189)	50.14 (9.50)	—

SOURCES: Data on Gulf War veterans from King et al., 2006; data on OIF veterans from Vogt et al. (2008); data on OIF and OEF National Guard and reserve service members from Renshaw (2010).

NOTE: Std = standard deviation.

[a] Difference from RAND sample (all contractors and PSCs only) is statistically significant ($p < 0.05$).

King et al.'s sample of Gulf War veterans speaks to the possibility that this finding may persist across other military populations as well. Of course, Gulf War veterans may have experienced worse living conditions while deployed than U.S. troops who have deployed in more recent conflicts. Future research should therefore endeavor to further examine contractor living conditions in relation to those reported by additional military populations.

Contractors reported feeling more adequately prepared for deployment on many of the individual DRRI items than did Chapman et al.'s sample of U.S. Army medics (see Table 3.7). However, we recognize that these comparisons may be prone to item-level variance, as responses to individual items are more likely to reflect errors than are aggregate scores on DRRI subscales or total scores. Therefore, all individual item comparisons presented here should be viewed as preliminary and exploratory.

To compare the reported combat exposure of contractors in our sample with military combat exposure, we looked to the reported combat exposure of a sample of 285 predominantly older National Guard and reserve OEF and OIF veterans from Connecticut (Pietrzak et al., 2011). In doing so, we found very little difference in reported combat exposure across each population on each of the individual DRRI combat exposure items that were common to both surveys, with the only statistically

Table 3.7
Comparing DRRI Preparation Individual Items, All Contractors, PSCs, and U.S. Army Medics

	% Who Agree / Strongly Agree		
DRRI Preparation Item	RAND Contractor Survey (all contractors)	RAND Contractor Survey (PSCs only)	OIF/OEF Medics[a]
I had all the supplies and equipment needed to get my job done.	66.6	67.7	68.0
The equipment I was given functioned in the way it was supposed to.	70.4	70.2	76.7
I received adequate training on how to use my equipment.	68.0	71.5	80.3
My contracting company provided me with adequate stress management training.	23.6	21.1	—
When I was deployed I had access to adequate resources to help with stress.	25.6	24.7	—
I saw as much combat as I expected.	50.5	52.4	19.6
I was informed about the role my unit was expected to play in the deployment.	76.9	80.7	55.6
When I was deployed I had a pretty good idea of how long the mission would take to complete.	76.5	79.4	51.2
When I was deployed I felt I had adequate administrative/logistical support for travel and mission requirements.	61.7	60.8	—
When I was deployed I felt that I had been prepared with adequate, accurate intelligence to support my mission.	54.3	53.1	—
I was accurately informed of what daily life would be like during my deployment.	61.3	59.7	40.6
I was adequately trained to work the shifts required of me during my deployment.	71.3	73.0	59.9

NOTE: Several items included in the DRRI deployment preparation scale as reported in Chapman et al. (2012) are omitted from this table because the RAND survey did not ask comparable questions of contractors.

[a] Data are from Chapman et al. (2012). All differences between contractors and U.S. Army medics are statistically significant at $p < 0.05$.

significant difference emerging between the two populations on the issue of encountering land or water mines or booby traps (see Table 3.8).

These comparisons of contractor and U.S. military deployment preparation, living conditions, and combat exposure contribute data to a vastly understudied issue thus far, but it should be noted that we modified the DRRI scales for our survey, and contractors were therefore asked a slightly different set of questions from those typically asked of military personnel. These comparative findings should therefore be considered as preliminary, exploratory, and deserving of further research.

Table 3.8
Comparing Contractors with OEF/OIF Veterans: Reported Combat Exposure

Experience	Contractors Number/Total Number (%)	OEF/OIF Veterans Number/Total Number (%)[a]
I went on combat patrols or missions.	—	164/272 (60%)
I or members of my team encountered land or water mines and/or booby traps.[b]	200/553 (36%)	124/272 (46%)
I or members of my team received hostile incoming fire from small arms, artillery, rockets, mortars, or bombs.	403/554 (73%)	200/272 (74%)
I was in a vehicle (for example, a truck, tank, armored personnel carrier, helicopter, plane, or boat) that was under fire.	216/548 (39%)	125/272 (46%)
I or members of my team were attacked by terrorists or civilians.	262/553 (47%)	144/272 (53%)
My team suffered casualties.	187/549 (34%)	82/272 (30%)
I was part of a land or naval artillery unit that fired on the enemy.	—	55/272 (20%)
Assaulted entrenched/fortified positions.	—	61/272 (22%)
My unit engaged in battle in which it suffered casualties.	—	82/272 (30%)
I personally witnessed someone from my team or an ally unit being seriously wounded or killed.	201/554 (36%)	96/272 (35%)
I personally witnessed soldiers from enemy troops being seriously wounded or killed.	—	102/272 (38%)
I was wounded or injured in combat.	—	42/272 (15%)
I fired my weapon at the enemy.	—	93/272 (34%)
I killed or think I killed someone in combat.	—	57/272 (21%)

NOTE: Response options to questions about combat experiences appear as worded in the survey, which used the modified DRRI combat exposure scale.

[a] Data from Pietrzak et al. (2011).

[b] Proportions are statistically significantly different ($p < 0.05$).

Conclusions

In our analysis, we found that the contractors in our sample reported being slightly better prepared for deployments than a previously studied population of U.S. Army medics, but contractors' perceived preparedness did not differ markedly from that reported by several other military populations in comparable studies. Contractors in our sample also reported comparable levels of combat exposure. Contractors' reported living conditions do appear to be significantly better than those reported by a sample of Gulf War veterans, however. Yet, because we used modified DRRI scales in our survey, there were slight differences in some of the questions asked of the contractor and military populations compared here. Therefore, these results should be viewed as preliminary, and point to the need for further research on this issue.

Our additional findings are as follows:

- There are statistically significant differences between U.S. and UK contractors on reported levels of preparation for deployment, combat exposure, and living conditions, with UK contractors reporting better preparation, lower levels of combat exposure, and better living conditions than U.S. contractors, on average. Moreover, citizens of countries other than the United States or United Kingdom reported even better preparation, less combat exposure, and better living conditions than UK contractors.
- Transportation contractors reported the lowest levels of preparation for deployment, the highest levels of combat exposure, and the worst living conditions of all job specialties. Meanwhile, logistics/maintenance contractors were best prepared for deployment and, along with maritime security contractors, reported the lowest levels of combat exposure. Logistics/maintenance and maritime security contractors also reported the best living conditions of all job specialties, though the bivariate analyses for living conditions by job specialty were not statistically significant.
- Shorter and more frequent deployments were correlated with higher reported levels of preparedness. Shorter deployments were also significantly correlated with lower levels of combat exposure and better living conditions.
- Contractors' age, prior military experience, and whether they carried a weapon as part of their job did not correlate with most deployment experience variables to a statistically significant degree, with one exception: Carrying a weapon was positively correlated with feelings of preparedness for deployment to a statistically significant degree.

CHAPTER FOUR

What Is the Mental Health Status of Contractors Who Work in Conflict Environments?

As noted in Chapter Two, the wars in Iraq and Afghanistan have brought significant attention to the effects of combat on the mental health of military personnel. In the United States, the prevalence of PTSD among returning service members is estimated at 5–20 percent (Ramchand et al., 2010); rates are reportedly lower in the United Kingdom, with cohort studies reporting a PTSD prevalence of 4 percent among UK military personnel who have deployed to Iraq or Afghanistan (Hotopf et al., 2006; Iversen et al., 2009) and 7 percent among UK military personnel with combat exposure (Fear et al., 2010). While it is likely that at least some portion of contractors in conflict environments face combat stressors and mental health problems that are similar to those experienced by military personnel, very little is known about the prevalence of deployment-related stress and mental health problems among the contractor population.

In this chapter, we present our findings on the proportion of contractors in our survey who met criteria for probable PTSD, depression, and high-risk alcohol use.[1] We also identify variations in those proportions by contractor specialty (i.e., job type), contract funder, citizenship, age, whether the respondent carried a weapon as part of his or her job, prior military experience, number of deployments on contract, and length of most recent deployment on contract.

Proportion of Contractors Who Met Criteria for Probable Mental Health Problems

Among respondents to our survey, 25 percent met criteria for probable PTSD,[2] 18 percent screened positive for depression, and 10 percent reported high-risk drinking (see Figure 4.1). The proportion of contractors who met criteria for PTSD or screened posi-

[1] As discussed in Chapter One, probable PTSD, depression, and high-risk alcohol use were assessed using standardized self-report scales.

[2] Our analysis showed that 20 percent of contractors surveyed had PCL-C scores of 50 or more, a common cutpoint that has been used in many studies. Twenty-five percent of contractors had PCL-C scores of 44 or more, a

Figure 4.1
Proportion of Contractors with Probable Mental Health or Substance Use Problems

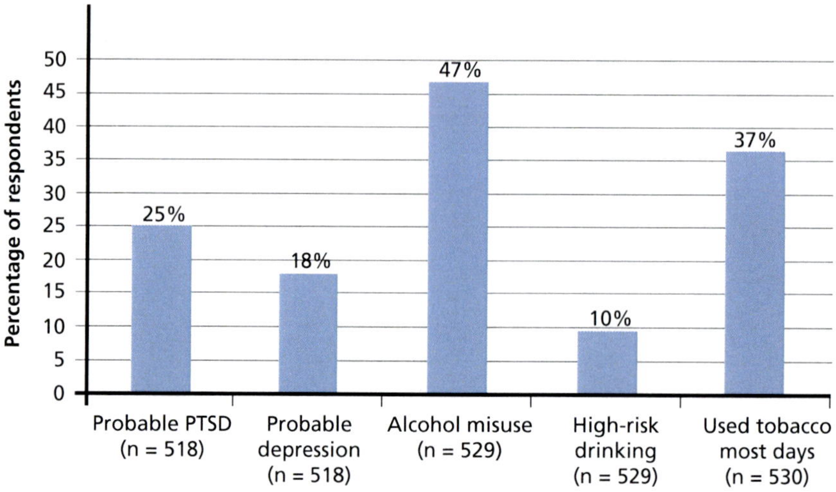

RAND *RR420-4.1*

tive for depression was notably higher than that among military populations, as discussed at the beginning of this chapter and in Chapter Two, although the proportion who reported high-risk drinking was similar to or lower than in military populations (Rona et al., 2010; Barlas et al., 2013). We also found high proportions of reported alcohol misuse (47 percent) and daily use of tobacco (37 percent). It is worth noting that while the methodologies and instruments used in previous studies are different—and, therefore, we cannot make a direct comparison—the proportion of contractors with mental health problems reported here is similar to those reported in previous studies (Feinstein and Botes, 2009; Miller, 2010a).

For the remainder of this chapter, we focus on our findings from the bivariate analyses of the relationship between contractor characteristics and deployment experiences with regard to probable PTSD and depression (see Tables A.4. and A.5 in Appendix A). We did not observe any differences in the proportion of reported high-risk drinking by contractor characteristic, including citizenship, or deployment experience.

There were significant differences in the proportions of probable PTSD and depression by job specialty (see Figure 4.2). Notably, half (50 percent) of transportation contractors who responded to the survey (n = 22) met criteria for probable PTSD. In addition, a third of contractors providing base support (32 percent) and training or advising services (31 percent) met criteria for probable PTSD, compared with 21–23 percent of contractors performing land security, logistics/maintenance, or management services, and less than 4 percent of maritime security contractors ($p < 0.001$).

---

slightly different cut-point that has been used in other studies (e.g., Bliese et al., 2007). Although less common, some studies use a cut-point of 30 or more, and 50 percent of contractors in our survey fell into this category.

Figure 4.2
Proportion of Contractors with Probable PTSD and Depression, by Job Specialty

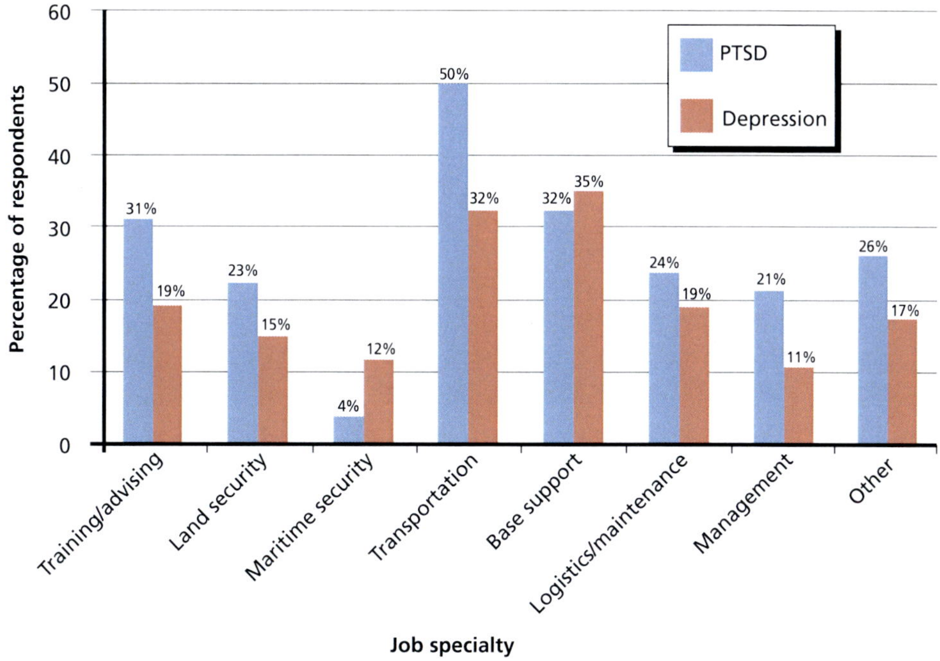

NOTE: As subsequent multivariate analysis indicated, these differences appear to be attributable to differences by job specialty in combat exposure, citizenship, or other factors. Nonetheless, to determine how best to target applicable mental health care initiatives for the contractor population, it is important to identify which job specialties have higher rates of mental health problems by virtue of higher levels of combat exposure (or other differences).

RAND *RR420-4.2*

We found similar differences for probable depression by job specialty, although these differences were not statistically different ($p = 0.05$). In post hoc analyses, we created logistic regression models predicting PTSD and depression and found that, after controlling for citizenship, military history, combat exposure, and other factors, job specialty was not a significant predictor of probable PTSD or depression (see Table 4.1). Thus, the differences we observed among job specialties are most likely due to differences in combat exposure, citizenship, preparedness for deployment, or other factors. For example, as described in Chapter Three, combat exposure differs by specialty (i.e., transportation contractors had higher levels of combat exposure), and combat exposure was a strong predictor of probable PTSD and depression.

We also found notable differences in the rates of PTSD and depression by citizenship (see Figure 4.3), with 32 percent of U.S. contractors meeting criteria for probable PTSD, compared with 12 percent of UK contractors (results are statistically significant at $p < 0.001$). Twenty-three percent of U.S. screened positive for probable depression, compared with 9 percent of UK contractors ($p < 0.001$). These differences persisted in multivariable regressions, which showed that U.S. contractors were 2.3 times more likely than UK contractors to meet criteria for probable PTSD (95-percent CI of 1.17–4.41) and 2.1 times more likely meet criteria for depression (95-percent CI of 1.03–4.46), controlling for job type, combat exposure, preparation for deployment, and prior military experience (see Table 4.1).

The citizenship differences in the proportions of contractors with probable mental health problems interestingly parallels differences by citizenship often found in the military mental health literature (Hotopf et al., 2006; Iversen et al., 2009) and in the general population literature. In epidemiological studies of general population samples, the prevalence of major depression, PTSD, and alcohol misuse vary widely by country. For each of these outcomes, the prevalence in the United States is among the highest among countries that have been studied. In an 18-country study of major depression, which used the same assessment instrument in each country, the 12-month prevalence of major depressive episode was 8.3 percent in the United States but ranged from 3.0–6.6 percent in the other high-income countries studied, with only two of the 18 countries (Brazil, at 10.4 percent, and Ukraine, at 8.4 percent) having a higher prevalence than the United States (Bromet et al., 2011). With respect to PTSD, the 12-month prevalence of 3.9 percent found in a nationally representative U.S. sample (Kessler et al., 1999) is very close to that found in a community study in the Netherlands (3.8 percent; Bronner et al., 2009), but it is substantially higher than in most countries in which the issue has been studied, including South Africa (0.7 percent; Atwoli et al., 2013), Germany (0.7 percent; Perkonigg et al., 2000), and Australia (1.3 percent; Creamer, Burgess, and McFarlane, 2001).

Figure 4.3
Proportion of Contractors with Probable PTSD and Depression, by Citizenship

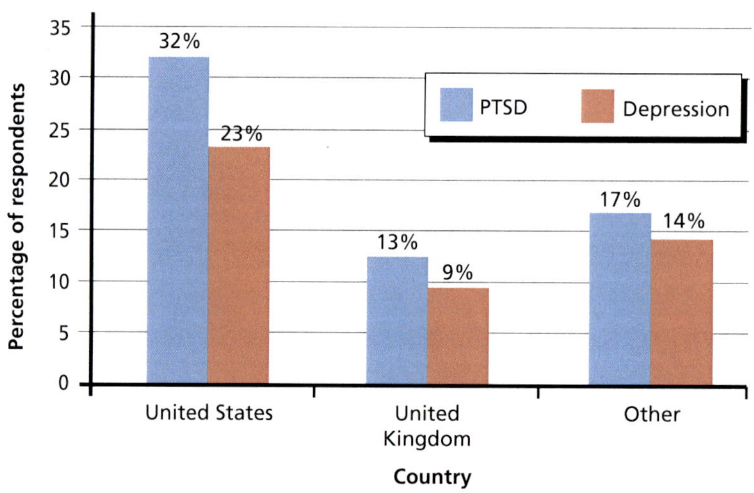

RAND *RR420-4.3*

A higher proportion of contractors who reported that their most recent deployment on contract had been funded by DoD met criteria for probable PTSD (32 percent) or depression (23 percent) than contractors funded by DoS (PTSD, 28 percent; depression, 21 percent) or another funder (PTSD, 18 percent; depression, 13 percent). (These results are statistically significant at $p < 0.001$ for PTSD and $p < 0.05$ for depression.) However, in logistic regression models predicting PTSD and depression, the most recent contract funder was not a significant predictor of probable PTSD or depression after controlling for citizenship (results not shown).

Similar to the literature on the effect of deployment length on the mental health of military personnel (Buckman et al., 2011), we found that longer deployments on contract were associated with higher rates of probable PTSD and depression (see Figure 4.4). Contractors who reported that their most recent deployment on contract was seven months or longer reported the highest rates of PTSD (44 percent) and depression (33 percent), compared with those with shorter contracts ($p < 0.001$ for PTSD and $p < 0.05$ for depression). Contractors who were deployed on contract at the time of the survey reported rates of probable PTSD (23 percent) and depression (33 percent) that were as high or higher than those who were no longer deployed. The observed differences in rates of mental health problems by length of deployment appear to be explained by differences in combat exposure, citizenship, or other factors (see Table 4.1).

As noted in Chapter Three, contractors reported moderate combat exposure (mean = 4.9 on a 0–24 scale), with rates of specific combat experiences similar to those of Iraq and Afghanistan veterans (Pietrzak et al., 2011). Combat exposure was associ-

Figure 4.4
Proportion of Contractors with Probable PTSD or Depression, by Length of Most Recent Deployment

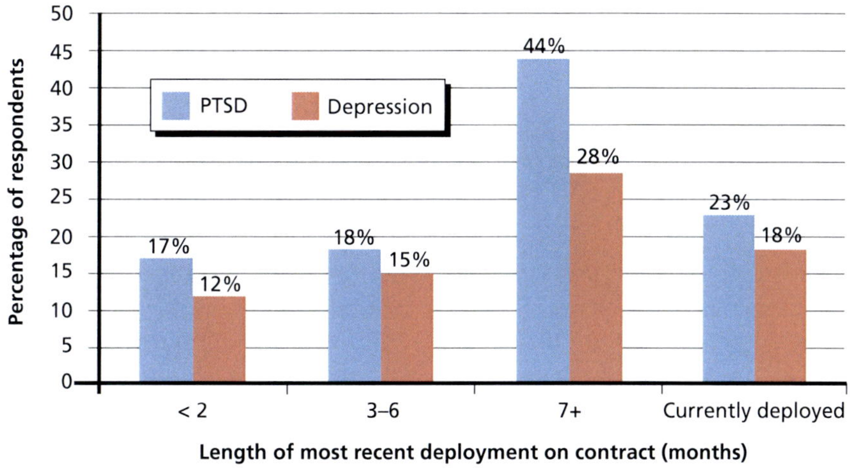

RAND *RR420-4.4*

Table 4.1
Predictors of PTSD and Depression Among Contractors

	PTSD (n = 481)		Depression (n = 482)	
Characteristic	OR	95% CI	OR	95% CI
Citizenship				
United States (reference)	—	—	—	—
United Kingdom	0.36[a]	0.17–0.75	0.42[b]	0.19–0.93
Other	0.71	0.33–1.50	0.85	0.39–1.88
DRRI preparedness items	0.85[a]	0.79–0.91	0.87[a]	0.81–0.93
Combat exposure	1.10[a]	1.06–1.15	1.08[a]	1.03–1.12
Specialty				
Land security (reference)	—	—	—	—
Base support	1.08	0.43–2.70	1.88	0.75–4.72
Logistics/maintenance	1.47	0.45–4.75	1.49	0.42–5.28
Management	1.06	0.36–3.14	0.64	0.17–2.43
Maritime security	0.21	0.05–0.97	1.52	0.52–4.28
Transportation	1.62	0.54–4.83	1.23	0.40–3.80
Training/advising	1.42	0.79–2.54	1.27	0.67–2.43
Other	1.02	0.43–2.41	0.91	0.35–2.35
Previous military experience	1.32	0.68–2.56	0.74	0.38–1.42
Length of most recent deployment				
< 2 months (reference)	—	—	—	—
3–6 months	0.47	0.22–1.02	0.79	0.34–1.84
7+ months	1.17	0.55–2.48	1.28	0.55–2.97
Currently deployed	0.63	0.31–1.27	1.18	0.54–2.57

[a] Statistically significant at $p < 0.01$.
[b] Statistically significant at $p < 0.05$.

ated with both PSTD and depression; contractors whose responses indicated probable PTSD had combat exposure scores that were 94 percent higher, on average, than those contractors who did not meet criteria for probable PTSD ($p < 0.001$). Similarly, contractors who screened positive for probable depression had combat exposure scores that were 70 percent higher, on average, than those who did not ($p < 0.001$). Controlling for citizenship, job type, preparedness, and prior military experience, the odds of having probable PTSD increased by 10 percent, and the odds of having probable depression increased by 8 percent with every one-point increase in combat exposure (see Table 4.1). Preparedness scores were negatively associated with probable PTSD (OR = 0.85) and depression (OR = 0.87) after controlling for citizenship, job type, prior military experience, and combat exposure ($p < 0.001$).

Conclusions

Individuals with recent deployments on contract to a theater of combat operations have rates of mental health problems that are comparable to or higher than those reported by members of the U.S. and UK militaries. Our specific findings are as follows:

- Twenty-five percent of contractors in our sample met criteria for probable PTSD, 18 percent screened positive for depression, and 10 percent reported high-risk drinking.
- We found significant differences by job specialty; in particular, 50 percent of transportation contractors met criteria for probable PTSD, compared with 32 percent of base support contractors and 4 percent of maritime security contractors. These differences appear to be explained by variations in combat exposure and other factors.
- A higher proportion of U.S. contractors than UK contractors met criteria for probable PTSD (32 percent versus 12 percent) and depression (23 percent versus 9 percent), and this difference persisted even when controlling for potential explanatory factors.
- Increased combat exposure was associated with higher rates of PTSD and depression, while increased reported preparedness for deployment was associated with lower rates of these mental health problems.
- These findings regarding the prevalence of PTSD and depression are very similar to those of two previous studies on the mental health of private security contractors (Feinstein and Botes, 2009; Miller, 2010a), despite differences in sample composition and methodologies for assessing rates of PTSD and depression.

CHAPTER FIVE

What Other Health Issues Affect Contractors Who Work in Conflict Environments?

As Chapter Four demonstrates, our survey respondents were screened on multiple measures of mental health and well-being. However, the literature reviewed in Chapter Two indicates potential links between a number of *physical* health issues and contractor deployments. Burn pits, for instance, are thought to pose a risk of serious respiratory problems, while IEDs encountered by contractors working on convoys or elsewhere have caused life-changing physical injuries and even death (Drummond, 2012; Pratt, 2011; Zajac, 2013).

In an effort to further explore the extent to which physical health problems affect the contractor population, this chapter explores the responses to three questions included on the survey: one asking respondents to rate their general or overall health, from excellent to poor; one asking respondents whether they had ever been diagnosed with a TBI; and one open-ended question asking respondents to describe any other health problems they believe they suffer as a result of a deployment on contract. We then explore correlations between physical health problems (as indicated by responses to these three questions) and job specialty, contract funder, citizenship, combat exposure, health insurance status, visits to a health care provider, and whether respondents had made a DBA claim (and, if so, the status of that claim). Moreover, because links between physical and mental health problems—including PTSD and depression—have been established among military populations (Jakupcak et al., 2008; Pacella, Hruska, and Delahanty, 2012), this chapter examines correlations between physical and mental health issues across our study sample.

Contractors' Overall Health Ratings Are Generally Positive

When asked to rate their general/overall health, the majority of respondents (69 percent) reported that their health was either "excellent" or "very good." One-fifth reported that their overall health was "good," 8 percent reported that it was "fair," and 3 percent reported that it was "poor," as shown in Figure 5.1.

Figure 5.1
Overall Health Rating

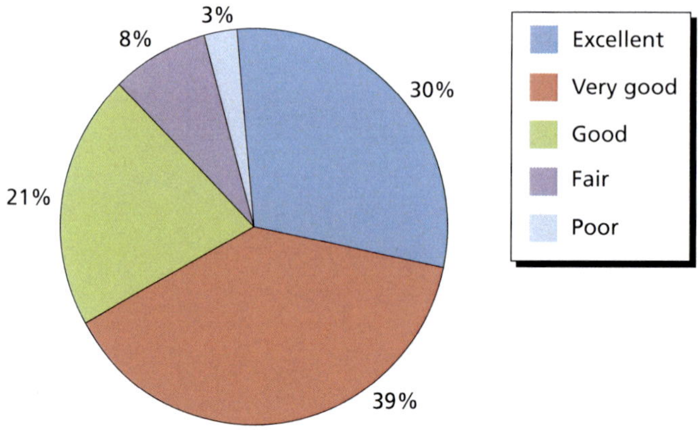

RAND *RR420-5.1*

Contractors Reported a Variety of Physical and Mental Health Conditions Experienced as a Result of Deployment on Contract

The prevalence of traumatic brain injury among military populations with combat deployments to OIF and OEF has been reported to be 8–20 percent (Hoge et al., 2008; Schell and Marshall, 2008, p. 87). Given that contractors in our sample reported fairly similar levels of combat exposure to those reported by military populations, we expected a fairly high level of reported TBI among the contractors sampled for this study. However, only 10 percent of the sample reported that a health professional had ever told them that they suffered from a TBI.[1]

Despite the fact that many respondents rated their overall health as "very good" or "excellent," 39 percent reported that they experienced a health problem that they believed was a result of their deployment on contract. Respondents were able to describe these health problems using up to 150 characters in an open-response box; responses were coded into the categories shown in Figure 5.2. Because this was an open-response question, respondents were able to list more than one condition, and the figure accounts for all conditions reported. As the figure illustrates, orthopedic injuries were by far the most commonly mentioned (by 75). Respiratory problems were also quite common (with 48 mentions), back pain received 38 mentions, and 34 respondents complained

---

[1] We note that this estimate may have been different if the survey question had been worded differently. Specifically, the question did not ask whether the respondent had sustained a concussion (mild TBI), which is the most common form of TBI. We also did not ask respondents when the TBI had occurred (i.e., whether they had received a TBI during their employment as a contractor). For these reasons, we present this data point as exploratory and do not include it in subsequent analyses.

Figure 5.2
Mentions of Health Conditions

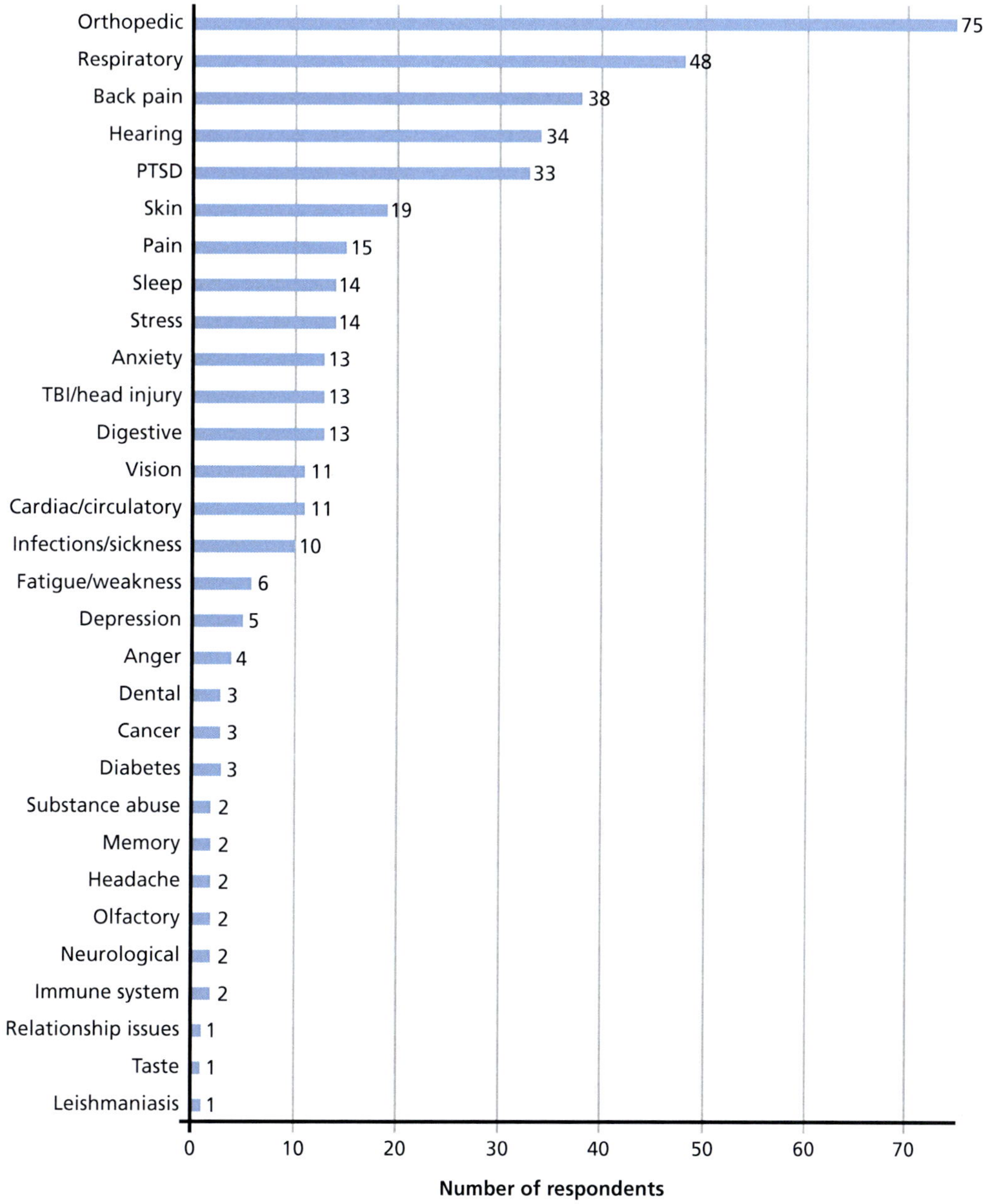

RAND *RR420-5.2*

of hearing problems. While mental health was screened separately in the survey and was discussed in greater detail in Chapter Four, it is worth noting that 33 people specifically complained of PTSD in the open-response box, 14 complained of stress, 13 complained of anxiety, five complained of depression, and four complained of anger.

In an effort to isolate physical health problems for analysis in this chapter, we assessed all responses to this open-ended question except for those citing *only* PTSD, anxiety, depression, or stress. We note, however, that certain other symptoms, such as sleep problems, may be indicative of mental health problems as well.

As noted earlier, we examined these responses across a number of variables. In doing so, we found that 55 percent of transportation contractors reported a physical health condition, compared with 47 percent of contractors in the "other" category, 43 percent of contractors engaged in training/advising, and 40 percent of land security contractors, as shown in Figure 5.3. While these findings are statistically significant ($p < 0.05$), the finding regarding transportation contractors should be viewed as preliminary and exploratory, as our sample comprised a low number of transportation contractors ($n = 22$). Meanwhile, maritime security contractors were the least likely of all of the job specialties to report a physical health condition as a result of their deploy-

Figure 5.3
Proportion of Contractors Reporting Physical Health Conditions, by Specialty

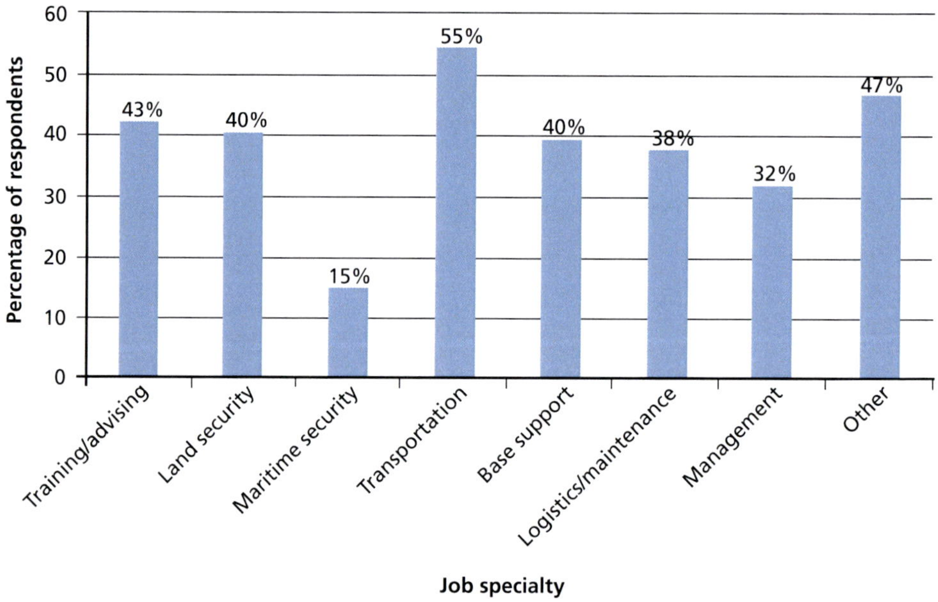

NOTE: As subsequent multivariate analysis indicated, these differences appear to be attributable to differences by job specialty in combat exposure, citizenship, or other factors. Nonetheless, to determine how best to target applicable health care initiatives to the contractor population, it is important to identify which job specialties have higher rates of health problems by virtue of higher levels of combat exposure (or other differences).

RAND *RR420-5.3*

ment on contract (15 percent). In an effort to determine the reasons for these differences, we conducted a multivariable analysis (see Table 5.1), finding that differences in citizenship, combat exposure, contract funder, length of deployment, and reported rates of probable PTSD or depression likely explain the differences in the observed rates of physical health conditions by job specialty.

Contractors working on DoD- and DoS-funded contracts were equally likely to report a physical health problem, with 46 percent of each group responding affirmatively. This is a relatively high proportion compared with contractors employed by other entities in the period from early 2011 to early 2013; only 30 percent of those working on contracts funded by entities other than DoD or DoS reported a physical health condition as a result of their deployment on contract. These findings are statistically significant ($p < 0.001$) and are illustrated in Figure 5.4.

One of the most striking of the physical health findings is the distinction between contractors of different nationalities (differences are statistically significant at $p < 0.001$). While 53 percent of U.S. contractors in the sample reported having a physical health condition as a result of their deployment on contract, only 16 percent of UK contractors did so. Meanwhile, 24 percent of contractors who were citizens of countries other than the United States or United Kingdom reported a physical health condition as a result of their deployment on contract (see Figure 5.5).

It is unclear why U.S. contractors are so much more likely than contractors of other nationalities to report a physical health condition. That said, U.S. contractors

Figure 5.4
Proportion of Contractors Reporting Physical Health Conditions, by Contract Funder

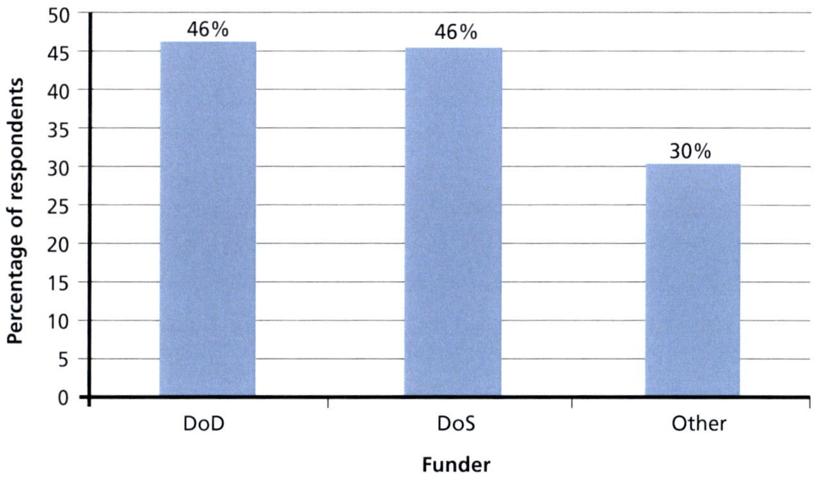

NOTE: The difference in rates of physical health problems by contract funder were not significant in the logistic regression model depicted in Table 5.1, once controls were added for citizenship, combat exposure, and other factors.

RAND *RR420-5.4*

Figure 5.5
Proportion of Contractors Reporting Physical Health Conditions, by Citizenship

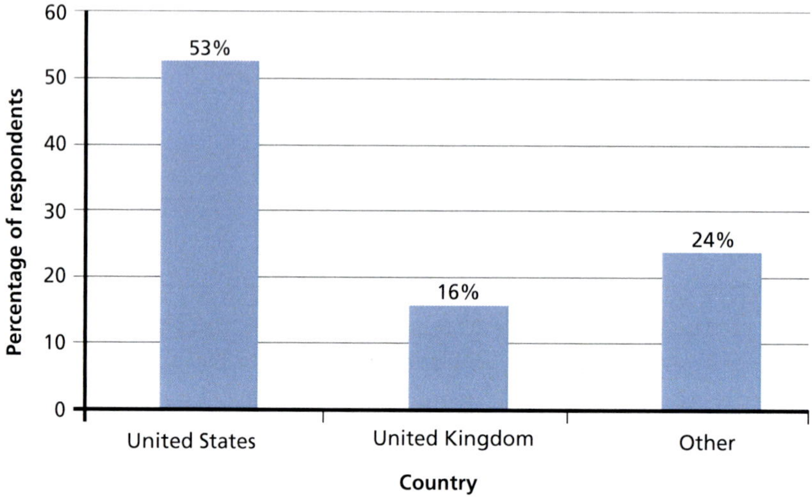

RAND *RR420-5.5*

also reported higher levels of combat exposure than contractors of other nationalities, were significantly more likely to work on DoD- or DoS-funded contracts, and were much less likely than UK contractors to perform maritime security functions. Additionally, UK citizens in the sample tended to report shorter deployments for their most recent contract (with 40 percent reporting their most recent contract deployment was less than one month), as did citizens of other nationalities (with 25 percent reporting their most recent contract deployment was less than one month). This is in stark contrast to U.S. citizens, 32 percent of whom reported recent contract deployments of more than 7 months and only 9 percent of whom reported deployments of less than one month. However, Table 5.1 details the results of a logistic regression demonstrating that even after controlling for specialty, combat exposure, contract funder, length of deployment, and reported PTSD or depression, contractors from the United Kingdom were still significantly less likely to report a physical health condition than were U.S. contractors (OR = 0.21).[2] It may be the case that U.S. contractors are exposed to more physically dangerous conditions on contract than UK contractors; additional research is warranted to explore this possibility. Another hypothesis that deserves further examination is that UK contractors may be less likely to report health problems than U.S. contractors due to cultural, societal, or other factors.

---

[2] Note that the difference between U.S. citizens and citizens of countries other than the United States or United Kingdom were not significant in the logistic regression model, shown in Table 5.1.

Table 5.1
Predictors of Physical Health Problems Among Contractors

Characteristic (n = 480)	OR	95% CI	P-Value
Citizenship			
United States (reference)	—	—	—
United Kingdom	0.213	0.108–0.420	0.00
Other	0.304	0.148–0.622	0.23
Specialty			
Land security (reference)	—	—	—
Base support	0.523	0.214–1.279	0.26
Logistics/maintenance	0.646	0.217–1.918	0.65
Management	0.795	0.301–2.101	0.99
Maritime security	0.706	0.264–1.889	0.78
Transportation	0.827	0.280–2.443	0.94
Training/advising	0.876	0.506–1.515	0.70
Other	1.219	0.544–2.731	0.22
Combat exposure	1.072	1.028–1.119	0.00
Probable PTSD	2.780	1.627–4.750	0.00
Probable depression	1.868	1.037–3.365	0.04
Contract funder			
DoD (reference)	—	—	—
DoS	1.018	0.579–1.791	0.51
Other	1.464	0.805–2.663	0.18
Length of most recent deployment			
Currently deployed (reference)	—	—	—
<2 months	0.464	0.235–0.916	0.02
3–6 months	0.987	0.558–1.748	0.38
7+ months	1.039	0.568–1.902	0.30

Contractors in the sample who reported suffering from a physical health condition as a result of a deployment on contract had higher combat exposure scores on the modified DRRI combat exposure scale (described in Chapter Three) compared with contractors who did not report a physical health condition ($p < 0.001$; see Figure 5.6). Indeed, in the multivariable regression presented in Table 5.1, increased combat expo-

Figure 5.6
Mean Combat Exposure Score, by Physical Health Condition

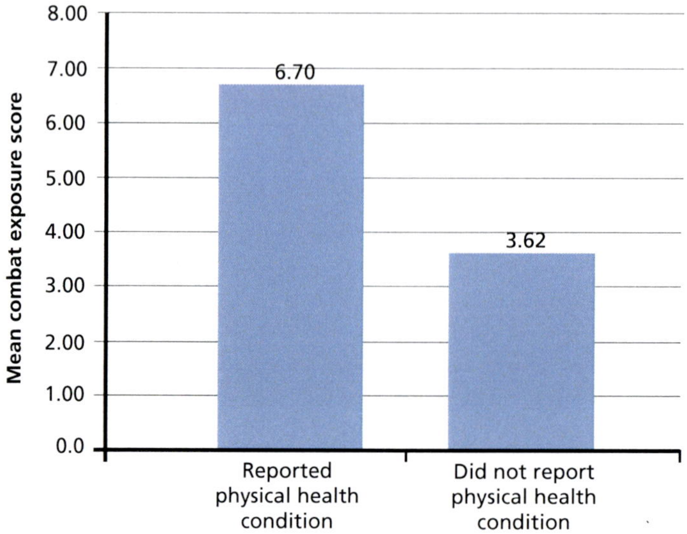

NOTE: Combat exposure scores range from 0 to 24, with higher scores indicating greater combat exposure.

RAND *RR420-5.6*

sure was significantly associated with having a physical health condition, even after controlling for other factors; for each one-unit increase in the combat exposure score, the odds of reporting a physical health condition increase by 7 percent. Although we were not able to examine causality, this finding lends support to a hypothesis that combat exposure increases the risk of developing physical health problems.

Rates of both probable PTSD and probable depression correlate fairly strongly with the presence of a physical health condition, as shown in Figure 5.7. Forty-three percent of respondents who reported a physical health condition screened positive for probable PTSD, compared with 13 percent of those who did not report a physical health condition ($p < 0.001$). Meanwhile, 30 percent of those who reported a physical health condition screened positive for probable depression, compared with only 10 percent of those who did not report a physical health condition ($p < 0.001$).

Conclusions

Although the majority of contractors surveyed reported that their general or overall health was either "excellent" or "very good," 10 percent reported that they had been diagnosed with a TBI, and 39 percent reported another health condition that they believed they suffered as a result of their deployment on contract. Respiratory prob-

Figure 5.7
Rates of Probable PTSD and Depression Among Those with and Without Physical Health Conditions

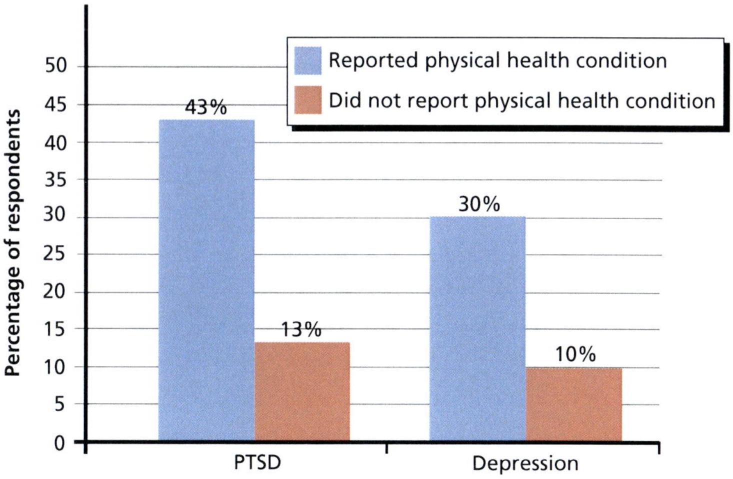

RAND *RR420-5.7*

lems, back pain, and hearing problems were the most common physical health conditions reported by contractors in the sample. A number of additional findings emerged from the bivariate analyses:

- Transportation contractors were the most likely to report a physical health condition (55 percent), compared with 47 percent of contractors in the "other" category, 43 percent of contractors engaged in training/advising, and 40 percent of land security contractors.[3] Only 15 percent of maritime security contractors reported a physical health condition as a result of their deployment on contract, making them the least likely of all of the job specialties to report a physical health problem. These differences appear to be explained by variations in combat exposure, length of deployment, and other factors.
- Contractors working on DoD- and DoS-funded contracts were equally likely to report a physical health problem, and both groups were significantly more likely to report a physical health problem than were contractors working on contracts funded by other entities.
- Fifty-three percent of U.S. contractors in the sample reported having a physical health condition as a result of their deployment on contract, compared with only

[3] Although these findings are statistically significant, the finding regarding transportation contractors should be viewed as preliminary and exploratory because our overall sample comprised few transportation contractors (n = 22).

16 percent of UK contractors and 24 percent of contractors who were citizens of countries other than the United States or United Kingdom. Even after controlling for specialty, combat exposure, contract funder, length of deployment, and probable PTSD or depression, contractors from the United Kingdom were still significantly less likely to report physical health conditions than were U.S. contractors. The underlying reason for this difference is unclear and deserves further examination.

- Contractors in the sample who reported a physical health condition as a result of a deployment on contract had much higher combat exposure scores than did contractors who did not report a physical health condition.
- Rates of both probable PTSD and depression correlate fairly strongly with the presence of a physical health condition.

CHAPTER SIX

To What Extent Do Contractors Access Health Care, and What Are the Barriers to Receiving Health Care?

In this chapter, we present findings from the survey that describe contractors' perceived access to and reported use of physical and mental health care, as well as reported barriers to receiving mental health care, in particular. We describe differences in perceived access and utilization by citizenship and health status (e.g., self-reported physical health problems, probable mental health problems) and also discuss findings on the perceived availability of company-provided resources for stress and mental health.

Access to Health Care

Because contractors in general, like those in our sample, represent different countries and work for a variety of companies on contracts funded by different sources, there is great variation in how and whether a contractor can access health care while deployed on contract and after the contract has been completed. Most companies provide medical care to contractors while they are deployed, and contractors working on U.S. government contracts are further able to obtain medical treatment at MTFs (Wise, 2012). Contractors who are citizens of countries with national health care systems (e.g., the United Kingdom) have access to health care regardless of employment status. contractors who are U.S. citizens or citizens of countries without national health care systems may access health care through other means, such as health insurance provided by a spouse's employer or other private or public health insurance.

Health Insurance

We asked the contractors in our sample whether they currently had health insurance and to what extent their company provided health insurance during and after a deployment on contract. As shown in Figure 6.1, we found that 83 percent of respondents were insured at the time of our survey. Thirty-eight percent were insured through their contracting company, while 14 percent were insured through another employer or their spouse's employer. A quarter (22 percent) responded that they had insurance from another source, and 10 percent indicated that the question was not applicable (i.e., they had access to national health insurance).

Figure 6.1
Current Health Insurance Status and Source

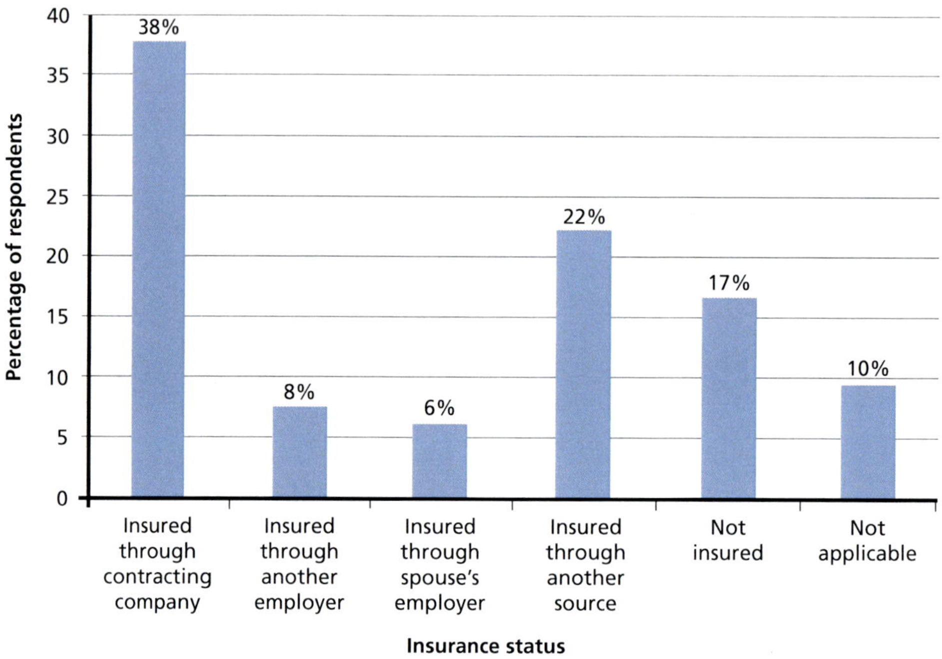

RAND *RR420-6.1*

The United States does not have national health insurance, so it is perhaps not surprising that a larger proportion of U.S. contractors reported being uninsured than those who were citizens of the United Kingdom (12 percent) or other countries (10 percent). As shown in Figure 6.2, fewer U.S. citizens reported receiving health insurance through their contracting company (31 percent) than did UK citizens (40 percent) or contractors of other nationalities (55 percent), but a much greater proportion of U.S. citizens (21 percent) reported receiving health insurance through another employer or their spouse's employer than did UK citizens (4 percent) or citizens of other countries (5 percent).

Most contractors (80 percent) reported that their company provided them with health insurance while they were deployed. Among those who reported receiving company-provided health insurance, 52 percent reported that this insurance covered them only during the deployment, while 28 percent reported that this insurance covered them for as long as they were employed by the company. There were no statistically significant differences in whether a contractor received company-provided health insurance during his or her deployment by funder of the most recent contract (chi-square = 0.77, p = 0.68) or by job specialty (chi-square = 11.80, p = 0.11).

Contractors with probable PTSD or depression were more likely to be uninsured at the time of our survey (22 percent) than were those without these conditions

Figure 6.2
Current Health Insurance Status and Source, by Citizenship

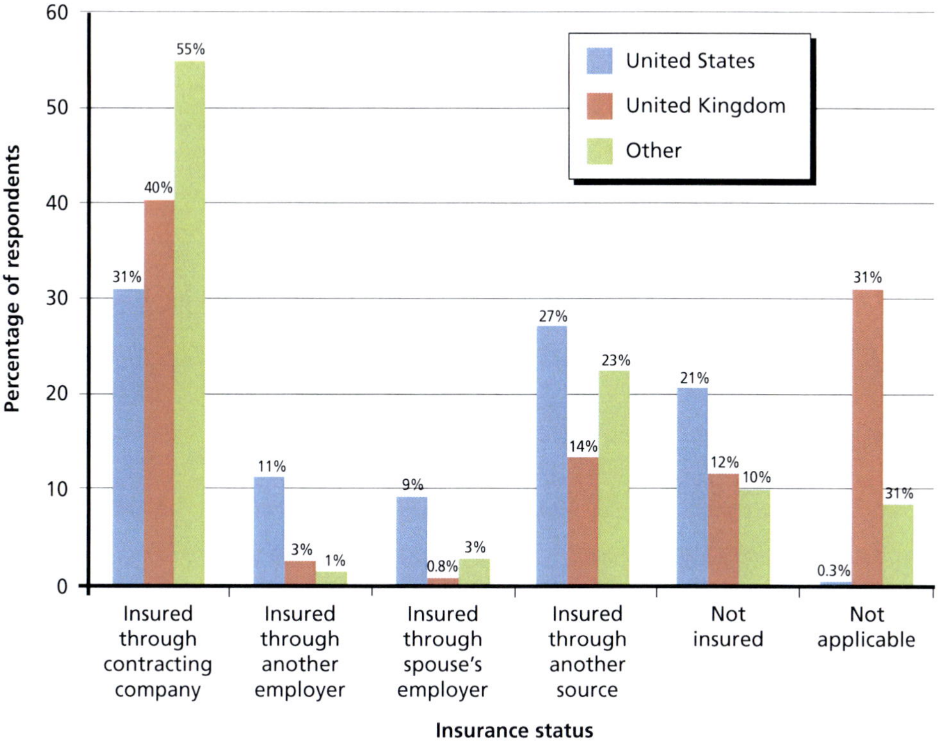

RAND *RR420-6.2*

(14 percent; chi-square = 8.86, p = 0.02); however, the majority of respondents with probable PTSD or depression reported that they currently had insurance (73 percent) and that their company provided them with health insurance while they were deployed (76 percent).

The majority (74 percent) of respondents who reported physical health conditions as a result of a deployment on contract reported that they had health insurance at the time of our survey, and a similar majority (76 percent) reported that their company provided them with health insurance while they were deployed. However, 55 percent of respondents who did *not* currently have health insurance reported a physical health condition, and 48 percent of those whose companies did *not* provide them with health insurance while deployed reported a physical health condition as a result of a deployment on contract. Figure 6.3 presents our findings for respondents with probable PTSD or depression or who reported a health condition and whether they were insured at the time of our survey.

Figure 6.3
Health Insurance Status Among Contractors with Probable PTSD or Depression or a Self-Reported Health Condition

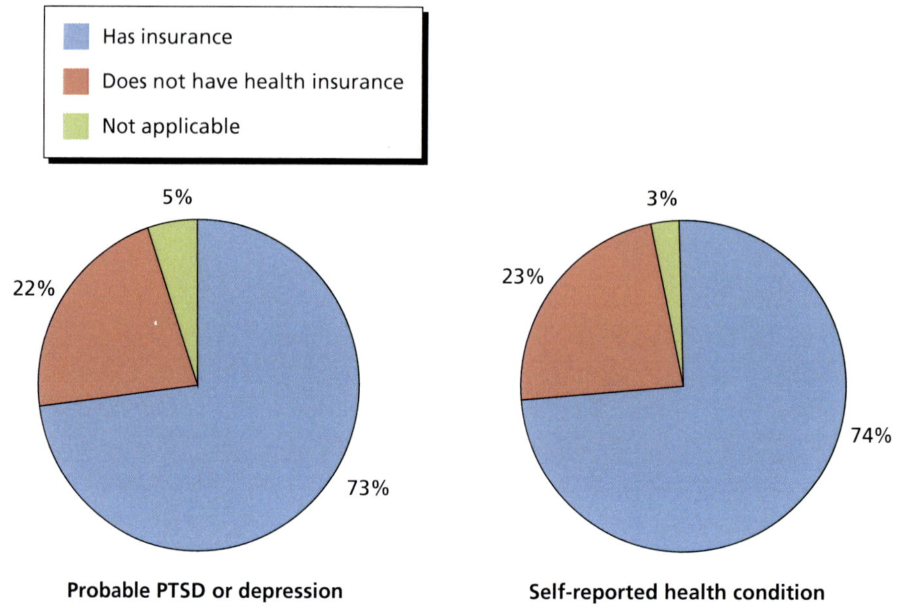

RAND *RR420-6.3*

Defense Base Act Claims

As mentioned in Chapter Two, the DBA mandates that all civilian employees working outside the United States on U.S. military bases or under a contract with the U.S. government for public works or national defense have access to workers' compensation for injuries or deaths sustained as a result of such employment. In theory, the DBA provides access to medical care for contract-related injuries and health problems, though media reports assert that this process is flawed and that many contractors with contract-related health problems have their claims denied (Miller, 2009a; Miller, 2009b). While we were not able to test this finding, we asked survey respondents whether they had ever filed a DBA claim and, if so, whether the claim was for a physical or mental health condition and whether the claim was approved or denied.

We found that 16 percent of respondents had ever made a DBA claim. Among those whose most recent contract had been funded by the U.S. government, 22 percent reported that they had made a DBA claim. As shown in Figure 6.4, the vast majority of DBA claims were for physical health problems (83 percent) rather than mental health problems (0.2 percent), although 14 percent reported that their claim was for both physical and mental health problems. A majority of DBA claims were approved (57 percent), which is surprising in light of the reports cited in Chapter Two. However, this apparent discrepancy with media reports on DBA denials may be explained by

Figure 6.4
DBA Claims and Reason for Claims

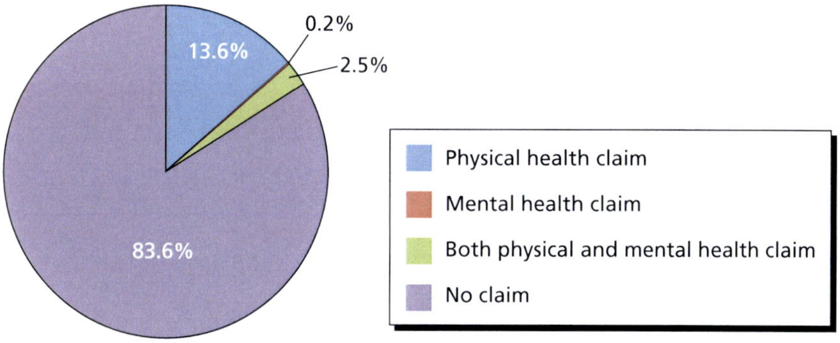

RAND *RR420-6.4*

the fact that almost a quarter (23 percent) of DBA claims were still being processed, and delays in DBA claim processing were also cited in reports on this issue. All in all, 37 percent of DBA claims were either denied or still being processed.[1]

Contractors from the United States were much more likely to file a DBA claim (24 percent) than were those from the United Kingdom (3 percent) or other countries (9 percent). Due to small sample sizes, we were unable to assess citizenship differences in DBA claim submission or approval status.

Of those respondents who reported a physical health condition, 68 percent reported that they had filed a DBA claim. Of those, 80 percent reported that they filed a DBA claim for a physical health problem, and 18 percent reported that they filed a DBA claim for both a physical and mental health problem. A slight majority (52 percent) of those DBA claims filed by respondents with a physical health condition had been approved.

Utilization of Health Care

We asked survey respondents about their health care use over the previous year. In particular, we asked how many times they had seen a health care provider (e.g., emergency room, primary care provider, family doctor, mental health provider) in the previous 12 months and, specifically, whether they had received any mental health treatment during that period. In general, contractors in our sample used health care relatively infrequently over the previous year. In our overall sample, more than a third (35 percent) of respondents had no health care visits in the previous 12 months, while about half (48 percent) had between one and three visits. Seventeen percent had four or more

---

[1] Six percent of respondents reported that they did not know the outcome of their DBA claim.

visits over the past year. Use of health care by this population appears to be lower than among the general civilian population in the Unites States; among individuals aged 45–54 (comparable to the modal age of the survey population), 17 percent had no health care visits in the previous 12 months and 45 percent had between one and three visits (National Center for Health Statistics, 2013). Given that the United States tends to have lower levels of health care use, on average, than other Western countries (Squires, 2012), it is likely that the difference between contractor and general civilian utilization of health care is even more pronounced in other countries.

Respondents reporting a physical health condition were more likely to report visiting a health care provider four or more times in the 12 months prior to the survey (28 percent) than were those who did not report a physical health condition (11 percent). As shown in Figure 6.5, half (49 percent) of those who reported a physical health condition had between one and three health care visits in the previous year, and a quarter (23 percent) of this group had no visits with a health care provider. Respondents who met criteria for probable PTSD or depression were also considerably more likely to visit a health care provider four or more times (33 percent) than were those who did not meet the criteria for these conditions (11 percent).

Contractors from the United States reported more visits to a health care provider in the previous 12 months than those from the United Kingdom or other countries (see Figure 6.6). More than half of contractors from the United Kingdom reported no visits to a health care provider in the previous 12 months. Nearly one quarter (24 percent) of

Figure 6.5
Number of Visits to Health Care Provider in Previous Year Among Those Who Reported a Physical Health Condition or Screened Positive for Probable PTSD or Depression

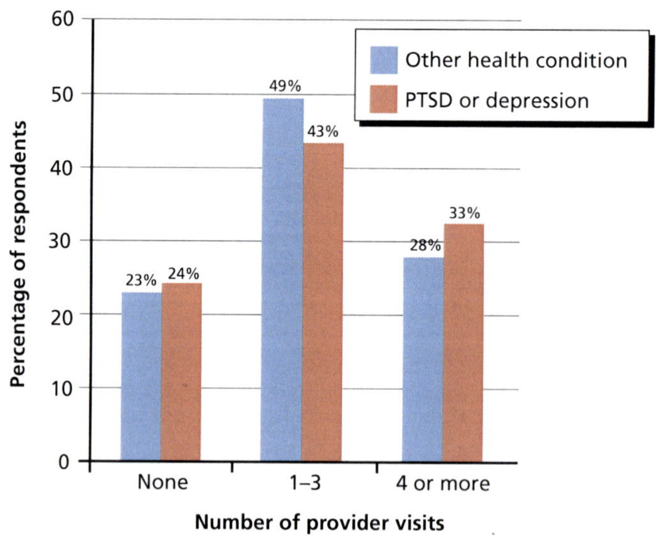

RAND *RR420-6.5*

Figure 6.6
Number of Health Care Visits in the Previous 12 Months, by Citizenship

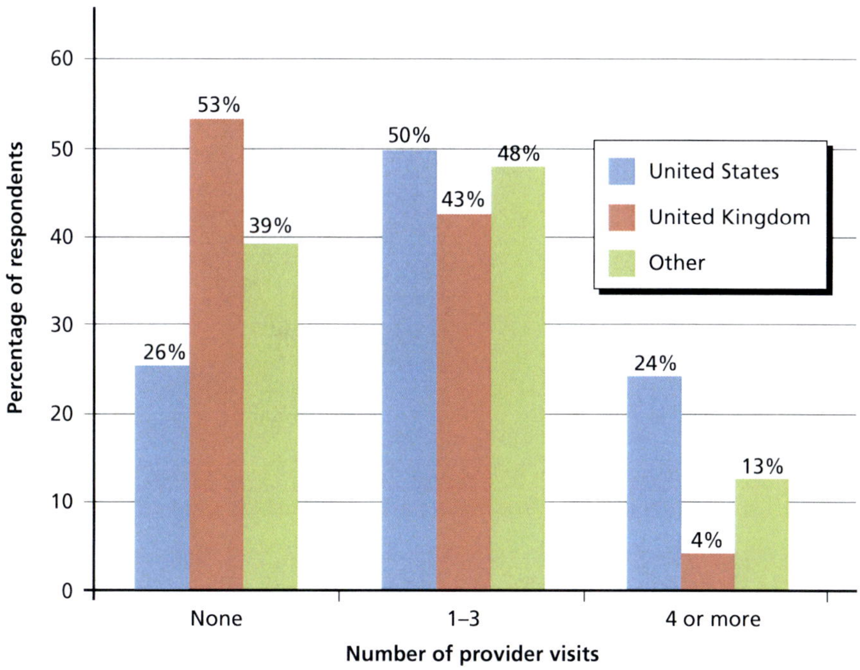

RAND *RR420-6.6*

contractors from the United States reported visiting a health care provider four or more times, compared with only 4 percent of contractors from the United Kingdom and 13 percent of contractors from other countries.

Ten percent of respondents had received some form of mental health treatment in previous 12 months. Among contractors who met criteria for probable mental health problems (probable PTSD or depression), 28 percent of those with probable PTSD and 34 percent of those with probable depression had received any mental health treatment in the previous 12 months (see Figure 6.7). We found some notable differences by citizenship: UK contractors were much less likely to seek mental health treatment in the previous 12 months (3 percent) than those from the United States (12 percent) or other countries (13 percent). Among those with probable PTSD or depression, 5 percent of UK contractors received any mental health treatment, compared with 25 percent from the United States and 40 percent from other countries ($p < 0.05$).

Access to Company-Provided Stress Management Resources

As discussed in Chapter Two, the contracting industry has made some effort to provide resources to mitigate the combat and operational stressors faced by contractors. Some

Figure 6.7
Receipt of Mental Health Treatment or Counseling Among Contractors with Probable PTSD and Depression

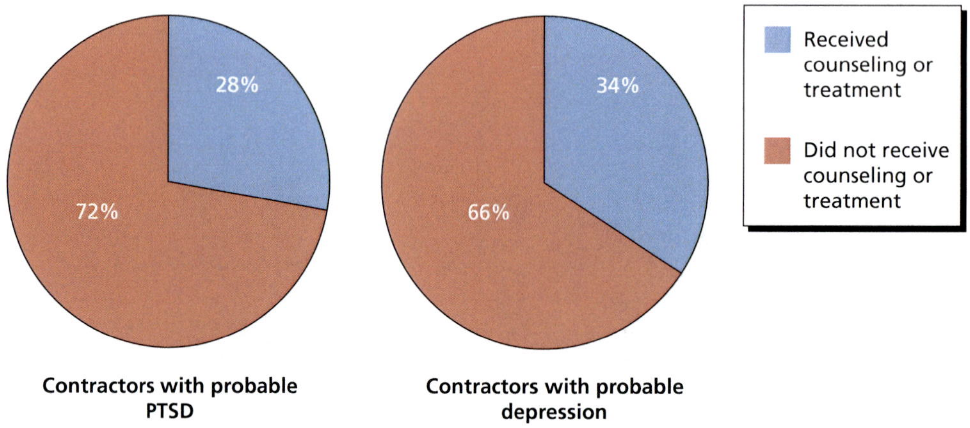

RAND *RR420-6.7*

companies have begun offering employee assistance programs, as mentioned in Chapter Two, which offer limited confidential counseling and referrals to employees. Other companies have contracted with consulting firms to provide training in combat and operational stress control and treatment or referral services for contractors with stress or mental health problems. To determine whether contractors perceived that such resources are available, we asked respondents whether their company provided them with adequate stress management training prior to their most recent deployment on contract and whether they had access to adequate resources to help with stress during a deployment. We also asked whether their company provided them with resources to help with postdeployment stress problems.

A minority of the contractors in our sample reported that they had access to company-provided resources to cope with stress before, during, or after a contract deployment (see Figure 6.8). Twenty-three percent somewhat or strongly agreed that their contracting company provided them with adequate stress management training prior to their most recent contract deployment, while a similar proportion (26 percent) somewhat or strongly agreed that they had access to adequate resources to help with stress during a deployment. Only 17 percent reported that their company provided them with access to resources to help with postdeployment stress.

We found no differences by contract funding source in the proportion of contractors who reported having access to company-provided resources to help with stress and mental health problems. However, we found that citizens of countries other than the United States or United Kingdom were more likely to report that they had received adequate stress management training (37 percent, compared with 21 percent for U.S.

Figure 6.8
Proportion of Respondents Receiving Adequate Stress Management Training and Resources

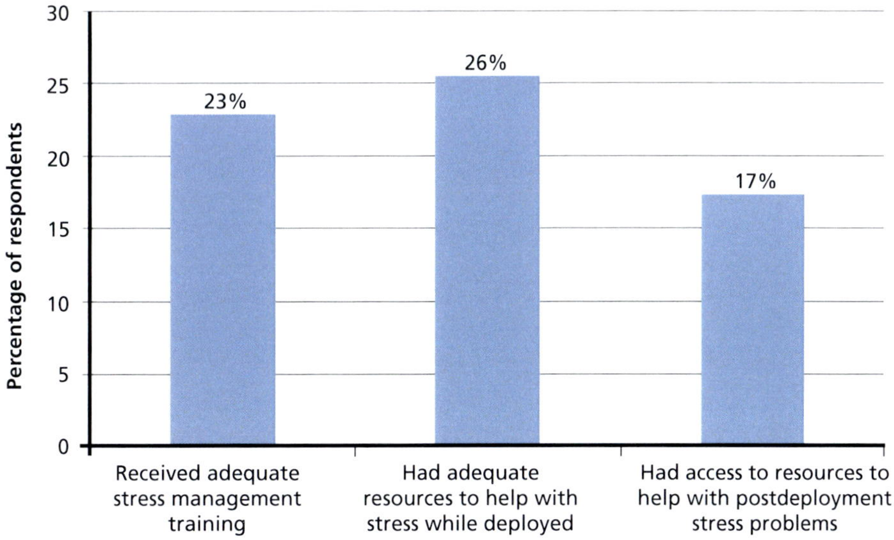

RAND *RR420-6.8*

contractors and 21 percent for UK contractors; $p < 0.05$) and adequate resources to help with stress while deployed (40 percent, compared with 24 percent for U.S. contractors and 25 percent of UK contractors; $p < 0.05$). There were no differences by citizenship in reported company-provided access to resources to help with postdeployment stress problems. While these findings are difficult to interpret, they do suggest that there may be a role for contract funders, especially the U.S. government, to influence access to resources to cope with stress and mental health problems, perhaps by requiring these resources as a condition of funding.

As shown in Table 6.1, access to company-provided stress management resources was strongly associated with probable PTSD and depression; for example, among those who received predeployment stress training, 13 percent had probable PTSD compared with 28 percent of those who did not receive such training ($p < 0.01$). After controlling for citizenship, job specialty, and combat exposure, predeployment stress training was still statistically significantly associated with rates of PTSD and depression (results not shown).

Perceived Barriers to Mental Health Treatment

Few contractors reported that transportation (6 percent), time (18 percent), or knowing where to get help (15 percent) were barriers to seeking mental health treatment. How-

Table 6.1
Access to Company-Provided Stress Management Resources

	Respondents with Probable PTSD		Respondents with Probable Depression	
Characteristic	**Number/Total Number (%)**	**P-Value**	**Number/Total Number (%)**	**P-Value**
Received adequate stress management training				
Yes	16/121 (13.2%)	< 0.01	6/120 (5.0%)	< 0.01
No	111/391 (28.4%)		86/392 (21.9%)	
Had adequate resources to help with stress while deployed				
Yes	15/137 (11.0%)	< 0.01	9/136 (6.6%)	< 0.01
No	114/376 (30.3%)		84/377 (22.3%)	
Company provides access to resources to help with postdeployment stress problems				
Yes	10/90 (11.1%)	< 0.01	4/90 (4.4%)	< 0.01
No	117/425 (27.5%)		88/426 (20.7%)	

ever, half of all respondents reported concerns about future employment as a barrier to seeking help, with 55 percent reporting that receiving mental health treatment would harm their career, 51 percent reporting that their colleagues would have less confidence in them, and 53 percent reporting that their supervisor or other officials at their company might treat them differently. Perhaps unsurprisingly, most contractors reported that they or their colleagues would be relatively unlikely to report a mental health condition to a supervisor or company official. On a scale of 1 to 10, with 1 being not at all likely and 10 being very likely to report a mental health condition, the average score was 3.8 (standard deviation = 2.8). Figure 6.9 shows the distribution of scores among all contractors in our sample.

Contractors who met criteria for probable PTSD or depression were more likely than those who did not meet these criteria to report barriers to receiving mental health treatment, as shown in Table 6.2. Among respondents with probable PTSD or depression, more than two-thirds reported concerns about future employment as a barrier to seeking treatment.

Figure 6.9
Likelihood of Reporting a Mental Health Condition to a Supervisor or Other Company Official

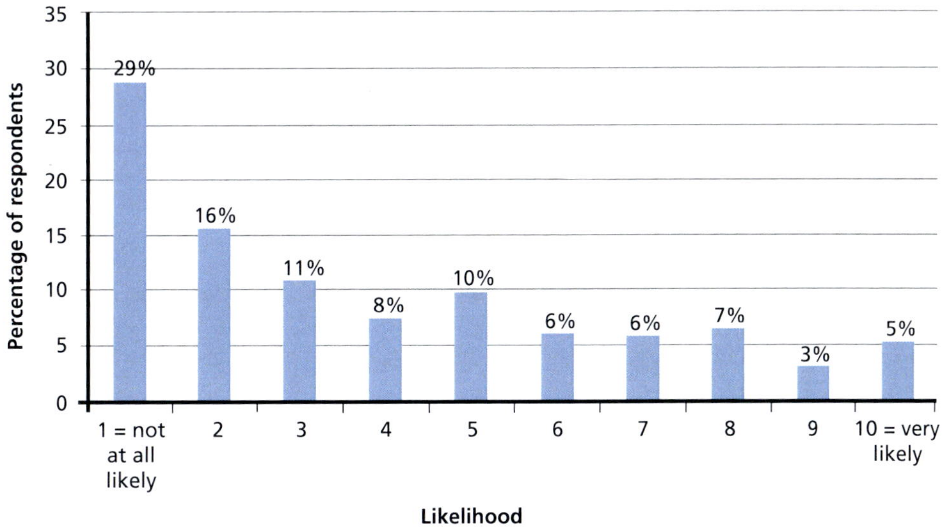

RAND *RR420-6.9*

There were few differences in perceived barriers to receiving mental health treatment by citizenship (results not shown), with the following exceptions:

- lack of trust in mental health professionals, with contractors from the United States more likely to cite this as a barrier (34 percent) than those from the United Kingdom (15 percent) or other countries (21 percent)
- cost, with contractors from other countries (45 percent) more likely to agree that cost is a barrier than those from the United Kingdom (17 percent) or the United States (36 percent)
- embarrassment, with 41 percent of U.S. contractors, 30 percent of UK contractors, and 23 percent of contractors from other countries in agreement
- belief that mental health care does not work, with 17 percent of U.S. contractors, 5 percent of UK contractors, and 11 percent of contractors from other countries in agreement.

The reasons for these differences by citizenship are not clear. One reason for the somewhat lower reported rates of embarrassment and belief that mental health care does not work among UK contractors may be a nationwide anti-stigma social marketing campaign, Time to Change, launched in England in January 2009. As of 2011 (the end of the first phase of the campaign), a general survey of UK residents revealed more positive attitudes toward people with mental health problems (Evans-Lacko et al., 2013) relative to responses to a baseline survey administered prior to the Time to

Table 6.2
Perceived Barriers to Mental Health Treatment

Response	Number in Agreement/Total Number (%)		
	Respondents with Probable PTSD or Depression (n = 159)	Respondents Without Probable PTSD or Depression (n = 360)	P-Value
I don't trust mental health professionals.	65/157 (41.4%)	73/352 (20.7%)	< 0.01
I don't know where to get help.	42/157 (26.8%)	32/349 (9.2%)	< 0.01
I don't have adequate transportation.	16/154 (10.4%)	15/351 (4.3%)	< 0.01
It is difficult to schedule an appointment.	41/157 (26.1%)	37/349 (10.6%)	< 0.01
There would be difficulty getting time off work for treatment.	42/157 (26.8%)	48/349 (13.8%)	< 0.01
Mental health care costs too much money.	78/157 (49.7%)	85/347 (24.5%)	< 0.01
It would be too embarrassing.	79/157 (50.3%)	97/349 (27.8%)	< 0.01
It would harm my career.	109/156 (69.9%)	171/350 (48.9%)	< 0.01
My colleagues might have less confidence in me.	107/157 (68.2%)	149/349 (42.7%)	< 0.01
My supervisor or other officials at my company might treat me differently.	111/156 (71.2%)	157/349 (45.0%)	< 0.01
My supervisor or other officials at my company would blame me for the problem.	69/157 (44.0%)	75/349 (21.5%)	< 0.01
I would be seen as weak.	103/155 (66.5%)	137/347 (39.5%)	< 0.01
Mental health care doesn't work.	28/157 (17.8%)	37/347 (10.7%)	0.03

Change campaign implementation (Evans-Lacko, Henderson, and Thornicroft, 2013). The success of this campaign among the general UK population could partly explain the more positive attitudes among UK contractors relative to those from the United States.

Conclusions

- Most (83 percent) of the contractors in our sample had health insurance at the time of our survey, but more U.S. contractors were uninsured (21 percent) than were UK contractors (12 percent) or those from other countries (10 percent).
- Most (80 percent) reported receiving health insurance from their contracting firm while deployed on contract, but, for the most part, this health insurance was limited to the period of deployment (52 percent) or to a limited time postdeployment (8 percent).

- A minority of contractors surveyed (16 percent) had ever made a DBA claim. Most DBA claims were approved (57 percent), although a not-insignificant proportion (37 percent) of DBA claims were either denied or still being processed at the time of the survey. Six percent did not know the outcome of their claim.
- In general, contractors in our sample used health care relatively infrequently over the previous year. More than a third (35 percent) had no health care visits in the previous 12 months, while about half (48 percent) had between one and three visits. Given that most contractors reported that they were in excellent or very good health, this may not be surprising.
- While contractors with self-reported health problems were more likely than those without health problems to have high health care use (four or more health care visits in the previous year), a quarter (23 percent) had no health care visits.
- There appears to be unmet need for mental health care: Only 28 percent of those with probable PTSD and 34 percent of those with probable depression received any mental health treatment in the previous 12 months.
- Half of the contractors in our sample reported that concern about future employment was barriers to receiving mental health treatment, and most would be unlikely to report symptoms of a mental health problem to a supervisor or other company official.
- Contractors who met criteria for probable PTSD or depression were more likely than those who did not meet these criteria to report stigma or other barriers to receiving mental health treatment.

CHAPTER SEVEN

Conclusions and Policy Recommendations

In an effort to fill the void of empirical research detailing the prevalence of mental and physical health problems among contractors working in conflict environments, this report described the results of the largest survey to date of contractors deployed to a theater of conflict between 2011 and 2013. The aim was to examine their deployment experiences, mental and physical health, and access to health care. The study produced a number of findings with potentially important policy implications.

Contractor Deployment Experiences Are Similar to Those of Military Populations but Vary by Nationality and Job Specialty

The analysis in Chapter Three of the deployment experiences of contractors in the sample showed that contractors' reported deployment preparedness and combat exposure did not differ markedly from comparable data on several different military populations. However, contractors' reported living conditions did appear to be significantly better than those reported by a sample of Gulf War veterans,[1] and their deployment preparation appears to have been slightly better than that reported by a population of U.S. Army medics.

We also found statistically significant differences between U.S. and UK citizens on reported levels of preparation for deployment, combat exposure, and living conditions, with UK contractors reporting better preparation, lower levels of combat exposure, and better living conditions than U.S. contractors, on average. Contractors who were citizens of countries other than the United States or United Kingdom reporting even better preparation, less combat exposure, and better living conditions than UK contractors. Transportation contractors reported the lowest levels of preparation for

[1] The degree of difference in scores between our contractor sample and a sample of Gulf War veterans (King et al., 2006) was significant enough to indicate that this finding may persist with regard to other military samples as well. However, because Gulf War veterans deployed more than two decades ago, and there may have been improvements in military living conditions in the ensuing period, further research should be conducted to compare the living conditions of contractors with those of troops deploying during the same period and in the same conflicts.

deployment, the highest levels of combat exposure, and the worst living conditions of all job specialties. Meanwhile, logistics/maintenance contractors were best prepared for deployment and, along with maritime security contractors, reported the lowest levels of combat exposure. Shorter and more frequent deployments were correlated with higher reported levels of preparedness, and shorter deployments were also correlated with lower levels of combat exposure and better living conditions.

Contractors Are Affected by Serious Mental Health Problems

Chapter Four built on our analysis of contractor deployment experiences to highlight that contractors with recent deployments to a theater of conflict had rates of mental health problems that were comparable to or higher than those reported by members of the U.S. and UK militaries. Indeed, fully one-quarter (25 percent) of contractors in our sample met criteria for probable PTSD, 18 percent screened positive for depression, and 10 percent reported high-risk drinking. By comparison, the prevalence of PTSD among returning U.S. service members has been estimated at 5–20 percent (Ramchand et al., 2010), while rates of PTSD are reportedly lower in the United Kingdom, with cohort studies reporting prevalence rates of 4 percent among UK service members who have deployed to Iraq or Afghanistan (Hotopf et al., 2006; Iversen et al., 2009) and 7 percent among UK personnel with combat exposure (Fear et al., 2010). It is notable that these findings regarding the proportion of contractors who met criteria for probable PTSD and depression are very similar to those in two previous studies of the mental health of private security contractors (Feinstein and Botes, 2009; Miller, 2010a), although there are significant differences among the studies in how PTSD and depression were assessed and in the characteristics of the sample populations.

We found significant differences in mental health by job specialty. Specifically, 50 percent of transportation contractors met criteria for probable PTSD, compared with 32 percent of base support contractors and 4 percent of maritime security contractors. These differences may be explained by variations in combat exposure. We also found differences by citizenship in mental health status, with a higher proportion of U.S. contractors than UK contractors meeting criteria for probable PTSD (32 percent versus 12 percent) and depression (23 percent versus 9 percent). Moreover, this difference persisted even when controlling for potential explanatory factors. The cross-national difference in the prevalence of mental health problems between U.S. and UK participants in this study mirrors that found in epidemiological studies of troops from the two countries (Sundin et al., 2010).

Longer deployments and increased combat exposure were both independently associated with higher rates of probable PTSD and depression, while higher reported levels of deployment preparation were associated with lower rates of these mental health problems. In addition, we found that rates of probable mental health problems were lower among contractors who reported having access to training and resources to cope with stress problems before, during, and after deployment on contract.

The mental health problems among contractors are particularly troubling given the large body of research concluding that PTSD is associated with significant impairment in occupational functioning and is likely to adversely affect contractors' on-the-job performance and need for medical care and long-term disability support. Epidemiological studies have found PTSD to be associated with a broad range of impairments (Holowka and Marx, 2012; Rodriguez, Holowka and Marx, 2012; Zatzick et al., 1997), including work productivity (Boscarino, Adams and Figley, 2006), employment (Smith, Schnurr and Rosenheck, 2005), and quality of life (Schnurr et al., 2009). Studies focused specifically on wartime trauma-related PTSD have reported similar findings: In a 2009 UK study, veterans with a score of 50 or higher on the PCL were two to four times as likely to report a work-related impairment than veterans with elevated but sub-threshold scores in the range of 40 to 49 (Rona et al., 2009). Notably, this study found that even sub-threshold PTSD symptoms were associated with occupational impairment; veterans with PCL scores of 30 or higher were more likely than those with scores below 30 to report problems functioning at work. Most troubling for the population of contractors working in conflict environments is the evidence that PTSD and alcohol misuse are independently associated with committing violent crimes after return from deployment (MacManus et al., 2012, 2013).

Contractors Also Suffer from Physical Health Problems

The analysis in Chapter Five found that although the majority of contractors surveyed for this study reported that their general or overall health was either "excellent" or "very good," 10 percent reported that they had been diagnosed with a TBI at some point in their lives, and 39 percent reported another health condition that they believed they suffered as a result of their deployment on contract. Respiratory problems, back pain, and hearing problems were the most common physical health conditions reported by contractors in the sample.

There were significant distinctions in physical health problems across job specialties in the sample, with transportation contractors most likely to report a physical health condition. In contrast, maritime security contractors were least likely to report a physical health condition as a result of their deployment on contract. Contractors working on contracts funded by DoD or DoS were equally likely to report a physical health problem, and both groups were significantly more likely to report a physical health problem than were contractors working on contracts funded by other entities.

We also found significant citizenship distinctions in reported physical health, following a pattern similar to that for mental health: Fifty-three percent of U.S. contractors in the sample reported suffering from a physical health condition as a result of their deployment on contract, compared with only 16 percent of UK contractors and 24 percent of those who were citizens of countries other than the United States or United Kingdom. Even after controlling for specialty, combat exposure, contract funder, length of deployment, and reported PTSD or depression, UK contractors were still significantly less likely than U.S. contractors to report physical health conditions. The underlying reason for this difference is unclear and deserves further examination.

Finally, contractors in the sample who reported a physical health condition as a result of a deployment on contract had much higher combat exposure scores than did contractors who did not report a physical health condition, and rates of probable PTSD and depression correlate fairly strongly with the presence of a physical health condition. The causes of the physical health problems reported in this study are unknown; for example, it could be the case that many of the physical symptoms reported are somatization of mental health problems, or it could be the case that contractors are exposed to physical risks (e.g., burn pits, mentioned earlier) that cause these problems. Additional research is warranted to understand both the scope of these problems and the potential causal factors.

Although Most Contractors Have Health Insurance, It Appears That Many of Their Health Care Needs Are Not Being Met

A fairly significant majority (83 percent) of the contractors sampled had health insurance at the time of our survey, but U.S. contractors were more likely to be uninsured (21 percent) than were UK contractors (12 percent) or those who were citizens of other countries (10 percent). Most (80 percent) reported receiving health insurance from their contracting firm while deployed on contract, though, for the most part, this health insurance was limited to the deployment period (52 percent) or to a limited time postdeployment (8 percent).

In general, the contractors in our sample used health care relatively infrequently over the previous year. More than one-third (35 percent) had no health care visits in the previous 12 months, while about half (48 percent) had between one and three visits. This finding is not surprising, given that most contractors reported that they were in excellent or very good health. However, while contractors with self-reported health problems were more likely than those without health problems to have high health care use (four or more health care visits in the past year), a quarter (23 percent) had no health care visits, indicating that there may be some unmet need for health care in this population.

We also found that a minority of contractors sampled (16 percent) had ever made a DBA claim. Among contractors whose most recent contract was funded by the U.S. government, 22 percent had ever made a DBA claim. Respondents reported that a slight majority of those DBA claims were approved (57 percent), although a not-insignificant proportion (37 percent) of DBA claims were either denied or still being processed at the time of the survey. As noted earlier, this finding provides a counterbalance to the media reports that most contractors' DBA claims are denied.

Finally, there appears to be an unmet need for mental health care, as only 28 percent of those with probable PTSD and 34 percent of those who screened positive for depression received any mental health treatment in the previous 12 months. Concern about future employability appears to play a role here, with half of contractors reporting that receiving mental health treatment would harm their career and that, as a result of receiving treatment, their supervisor or other company officials would treat them differently. Contractors who met criteria for probable PTSD or depression were more likely than those who did not meet these criteria to report concerns about future employability and other barriers to receiving mental health treatment.

Policy Recommendations

Increase Access to Stress Management and Mental Health Resources

Contractors infrequently receive training in stress management prior to a combat deployment, and few company-provided resources are available to them during or after a combat deployment. Indeed, we found that significantly fewer contractors who had access to such resources met criteria for probable PTSD or depression compared with those who did not have access to such resources. While we are not able to assess causality in a cross-sectional study, this finding does suggest that private contracting firms may wish to consider providing these resources more uniformly. In addition, funding agents issuing these contracts, such as DoD, might consider requiring that contractor personnel have access to stress and mental health resources as a condition of the contract. Funding agents might also consider incorporating coverage requirements for the mental and/or physical health care of contractor employees, either during or after deployment, directly into contract provisions and costs at the outset. Future research is needed to explore the economic impact of such contract provisions, including their impact on the health insurance market for contractors.

Reduce Barriers to Seeking Treatment for Mental Health Problems

The perception of stigma when it comes to seeking mental health care and concerns about future employability appear to pose a considerable barrier to contractors who need such care. On average, roughly twice as many contractors with probable PTSD or depression agreed with statements about stigmatization of mental health care and barriers to care, as did contractors without probable mental health conditions. Reluctance to seek help for fear of being stigmatized is not an issue unique to contractors. As discussed in Chapter Two, U.S. and UK service members are reluctant to seek help for various reasons (Evans-Lacko, Henderson, and Thornicroft, 2013; Iversen et al., 2011).

General population surveys indicate that the general civilian population is also fearful of negative outcomes as a result of seeking treatment (Mojtabai, 2007; Substance Abuse and Mental Health Services Administration, 2012).

There are several policy options to help companies reduce barriers to seeking mental health treatment, including increasing awareness about stress and mental health problems associated with contract deployment, providing training to team leaders to identify and normalize stress reactions, and providing access to confidential counseling.

In general, two broad strategies—education and providing contact with people with mental health problems—have been found to be successful in reducing mental health care stigma (Collins et al., 2012; Penn and Couture, 2002; Thornicroft et al., 2008). These strategies are often combined into programs and presentations in which educational information is presented, and people with mental health challenges serve as presenters and speak about their experiences (e.g., the National Alliance for the Mentally Ill In Our Own Voices Program in the United States). Broad social marketing campaigns aiming to both educate and provide contact with people with mental illness have been implemented for the general population (e.g., the United Kingdom's Time to Change, Defeat Depression, and Changing Minds campaigns). Similar campaigns have targeted military and veteran populations (e.g., the National Center for PTSD's About Face campaign in the United States). Formal evaluations of Time to Change (Evans-Lacko, Henderson, and Thornicroft, 2013; Evans-Lacko et al., 2013), Defeat Depression (Paykel, Hart, and Priest, 1998), and Changing Minds (Crisp et al., 2005) show positive changes in attitudes toward mental health. To our knowledge, the About Face campaign has not been evaluated.

DoD has also implemented a number of policies, programs, and initiatives to reduce mental health care stigma, which may provide some guidance for companies in designing similar efforts. First, DoD has written policies on the responsibility of commanders to reduce stigma. For example, DoD Instruction 6490.08 (2011) states, "Commanders must also reduce stigma through positive regard for those who seek mental health assistance to restore and maintain their mission readiness, just as they would view someone seeking treatment for any other medical issue." Such policies can help by providing clear guidance on the responsibility of leadership to reduce stigma. Second, DoD has launched programs, such as the Real Warriors Campaign,[2] that aim to reduce stigma by providing information, testimony from service members (including high-ranking officers) who have experienced mental health problems, and resources for finding help. In the United Kingdom, the Ministry of Defence has launched the Trauma Risk Management program, which provides training to unit leaders in identifying and responding to personnel who have been exposed to trauma and stress or

---

[2] The Real Warriors Campaign is a multimedia public awareness campaign designed to encourage help-seeking behavior among service members with mental health problems.

are exhibiting signs of mental health problems. Evidence suggests that attitudes toward stress and mental health problems, as well as help-seeking for those problems, improve among personnel who have received the training (Gould, Greenberg, and Hetherton, 2007).

Similar approaches may be appropriate for the contracting community and could even be a joint effort among several contracting firms or funders.

Conduct Additional Research to Better Understand the Needs of This Population

This study is the largest and most comprehensive of its kind to date, but it is nonetheless intended as an exploratory examination of the prevalence of mental and physical health problems among a broad population of contractors who work in conflict environments and barriers to contractors' access to mental health services. The findings presented here strongly indicate a need for additional research in a number of areas.

First, additional research is necessary to more thoroughly identify the experiences and characteristics of contractors that may be associated with mental health problems. For example, because the majority of contractors have prior military experience, it is important to understand how this prior experience (e.g., combat and trauma exposure during deployments) affects contractors' mental health. Relatedly, understanding how prior military experiences may have shaped contractors' perceptions about mental health and mental health care could help to inform efforts to reduce stigma among this population. A better understanding of the types of stress and mental health resources that companies provide to contractors, and the extent to which these resources can prevent negative consequences in this population, could inform efforts to expand the availability of such resources. Additional research is also warranted to clarify the relationship between mental health problems and occupational functioning in this population. To date, research on the relationship between PTSD and functional impairment has focused on military service members and veterans with PTSD diagnoses; much less is known about the effect of sub-threshold PTSD symptoms on job performance. Given that a high proportion of contractors in our study reported sub-threshold PTSD symptoms, the possible occupational consequences will be an important topic for future study.

Second, this study focused in great detail on contractors' mental health and well-being, exploring physical health and well-being in more general terms. More focused, detailed research on the physical health problems that contractors face as a result of deployment, the causes of these problems, and any barriers to accessing physical health services is therefore warranted. As noted in Chapter Three, further research is also needed to better identify how contractors' deployment experiences compare with those of military personnel, how these experiences shape contractor health and well-being, and how contractors' outcomes compare with those of their military counterparts.

Third, we found significant distinctions by citizenship in each of the main lines of inquiry in our study. Even when controlling for a number of other potentially causal variables in logistic regression models, these distinctions by citizenship persisted, leading us to conclude that further research is needed to determine the underlying causes for these differences.

Fourth, future research that samples a larger population of contractors in specific job specialties of interest would be a valuable contribution to the current body of knowledge. Future research into the health and well-being of transportation or logistics/maintenance contractors is warranted, given the interesting preliminary findings about these groups, in particular.

This study points to several lessons to keep in mind when designing and conducting further research into these or related topics. As noted in Chapter One, one of the challenges to studying the entire transnational population of contractors operating in conflict environments globally is the inherent difficulty in specifying a sampling frame. While we endeavored to overcome this challenge by distributing this study's survey widely and comparing our survey sample with other known quantitative data on certain specified populations of contractors (such as those operating on DoD contracts during a particular time frame), future research should incorporate alternative mechanisms to identify a more clearly representative sample of this broad population.

Perhaps most importantly, because the height of contracting in recent years occurred during the 2005–2011 period in both Iraq and Afghanistan, future research should aim to provide a more comprehensive picture of the health and well-being of all contractors deployed over the past decade. As we note in Chapter One, if contractors who deployed prior to 2011 had been allowed to participate in this study, the prevalence of health problems among this population might appear to be higher.

Conclusions

Although contractors have become a nontrivial part of the fighting force in several theaters of conflict over the past decade, their characteristics, deployment experiences, and health status have not been thoroughly explored. This study found that the contractors sampled have similar deployment experiences to military personnel—including combat exposure. The contractors in our study reported relatively high rates of probable mental health problems, including PTSD and depression. Moreover, our findings suggest that this population has few resources to cope with these problems and faces significant barriers to seeking mental health treatment. In addition, the contractors sampled attributed physical health problems to their employment on contract; this finding warrants additional attention in future research studies.

The findings presented in this report will likely be of interest to a variety of audiences. The majority of contractors are military veterans, so policymakers in the United States, United Kingdom, and other countries who are concerned with the success and well-being of veterans likely have an interest in ensuring that veterans who are contractors have access to needed mental and physical health resources. Additionally, in an effort to ensure the continued availability of a healthy workforce and reduce the risk of negative consequences associated with undetected and untreated health problems, contract funders—including national governments—and contracting firms would benefit from a better understanding of the health challenges facing contractors and their potential solutions.

APPENDIX A

Additional Data Tables

Table A.1
Reported Levels of Preparation for Deployment on Contract

Characteristic	Mean Score	Overall F-Test or T-Test (p-value)
Specialty		
Training/advising (n = 135)	6.88	3.19 (0.00)
Land security (n = 220)	7.20	
Maritime security (n = 58)	8.21	
Transportation (n = 24)	5.45	
Base support (n = 45)	5.95	
Logistics/maintenance (n = 24)	8.17	
Management (n = 37)	7.66	
Other (n = 66)	6.43	
Contract funder		
DoD (n = 186)	6.82	3.11 (0.05)
DoS (n = 131)	6.63	
Other (n = 263)	7.44	
Citizenship		
United States (n = 300)	6.66	7.50 (0.00)
United Kingdom (n = 119)	7.24	
Other (n = 71)	8.37	
Age		
Under 40 (n = 170)	7.17	0.66 (0.51)
40 or older (n = 337)	6.96	

Table A.1—Continued

Characteristic	Mean Score	Overall F-Test or T-Test (p-value)
Carried a weapon as part of job		
Yes (n = 379)	7.29	2.44 (0.02)
No (n = 192)	6.55	
Previous military experience		
Yes (n = 488)	7.10	0.80 (0.42)
No (n = 91)	6.79	
Length of most recent contract		
< 2 months (n = 140)	7.87	3.84 (0.01)
3–6 months (n = 129)	6.98	
7+ months (n = 120)	6.72	
Currently deployed (n = 189)	6.68	
Number of deployments on contract		
1 (n = 117)	6.51	6.63 (0.00)
2 (n = 86)	6.22	
3 or more (n = 373)	7.45	

Table A.2
Reported Levels of Combat Exposure During Deployment on Contract

Characteristic	Mean Score	Overall F-Test (p-value)
Specialty		
Training/advising (n = 149)	5.41	3.20 (0.00)
Land security (n = 251)	5.02	
Maritime security (n = 63)	3.05	
Transportation (n = 25)	8.78	
Base support (n = 45)	4.27	
Logistics/maintenance (n = 24)	3.02	
Management (n = 37)	5.26	
Other (n = 66)	4.50	

Table A.2—Continued

Characteristic	Mean Score	Overall F-Test (p-value)
Contract funder		
DoD (n = 184)	5.56	2.27 (0.10)
DoS (n = 129)	4.29	
Other (n = 246)	4.76	
Citizenship		
United States (n = 299)	5.52	5.29 (0.01)
United Kingdom (n = 113)	3.90	
Other (n = 71)	3.80	
Age		
Under 40 (n = 167)	5.50	1.01 (0.92)
40 or older (n = 333)	5.47	
Carried a weapon as part of job		
Yes (n = 367)	5.10	1.03 (0.30)
No (n = 184)	4.59	
Previous military experience		
Yes (n = 470)	5.06	1.42 (0.16)
No (n = 88)	4.26	
Length of most recent contract		
< 2 months	3.35	11.67 (0.00)
3–6 months	5.29	
7+ months	7.19	
Currently deployed.	4.35	
Number of deployments on contract		
1 (n = 112)	4.29	1.05 (0.35)
2 (n = 84)	5.40	
3 or more (n = 359)	4.97	

Table A.3
Living Conditions While Deployed on Contract

Characteristic	Mean Score	Overall F-Test (p-value)
Specialty		
Training/advising (n = 127)	11.87	1.63 (0.12)
Land security (n = 202)	12.31	
Maritime security (n = 53)	12.95	
Transportation (n = 22)	10.36	
Base support (n = 39)	12.10	
Logistics/maintenance (n = 21)	12.52	
Management (n = 28)	12.06	
Other (n = 47)	11.92	
Contract funder		
DoD (n = 175)	11.8	3.21 (0.04)
DoS (n = 124)	11.8	
Other (n = 239)	12.5	
Citizenship		
United States (n = 300)	11.6	12.28 (0.00)
United Kingdom (n = 120)	12.9	
Other (n = 70)	13.3	
Age		
Under 40 (n = 170)	11.9	1.17 (0.22)
40 or older (n = 337)	12.3	
Carried a weapon as part of job		
Yes (n = 357)	12.2	0.25 (0.80)
No (n = 174)	12.1	
Previous military experience		
Yes (n = 542)	12.1	-0.18 (0.86)
No (n = 104)	12.2	

Table A.3—Continued

Characteristic	Mean Score	Overall F-Test (p-value)
Length of most recent contract		
< 2 months (n = 126)	13.1	5.90 (0.00)
3–6 months (n = 121)	11.8	
7+ months (n = 113)	11.4	
Currently deployed (n = 177)	12.2	
Number of deployments on contract		
1 (n = 107)	12.1	1.86 (0.16)
2 (n = 82)	11.5	
3 or more (n = 346)	12.3	

Table A.4
Proportion of Contractors with Probable PTSD

Characteristic	Number (%)	Chi-Square (p-value)
Specialty		
Training/advising (n = 125)	39 (31.2%)	24.3 (0.00)
Land security (n = 187)	42 (22.5%)	
Maritime security (n = 52)	2 (3.9%)	
Transportation (n = 22)	11 (50.0%)	
Base support (n = 37)	12 (32.4%)	
Logistics/maintenance (n = 21)	5 (23.8%)	
Management (n = 28)	6 (21.4%)	
Other (n = 46)	12 (26.1%)	
Contract funder		
DoD (n = 169)	54 (32.0%)	10.8 (0.00)
DoS (n = 121)	34 (28.1%)	
Other (n = 227)	41 (18.1%)	
Citizenship		
United States (n = 299)	96 (32.1%)	20.48 (0.00)
United Kingdom (n = 120)	15 (12.5%)	
Other (n = 71)	12 (16.9%)	

Table A.4—Continued

Characteristic	Number (%)	Chi-Square (p-value)
Age		
Under 40 (n = 169)	42 (24.9%)	0.01 (0.94)
40 or older (n = 338)	85 (25.2%)	
Previous military experience		
Yes (n = 437)	108 (24.7%)	0.08 (0.77)
No (n = 80)	21 (26.3%)	
Carried a weapon as part of job		
Yes (n = 341)	78 (22.9%)	2.7 (0.10)
No (n = 169)	50 (29.6%)	
Number of deployments on contract		
1 (n = 105)	25 (23.8%)	3.82 (0.15)
2 (n = 77)	26 (33.8%)	
3 or more (n = 332)	77 (23.2%)	
Length of most recent contract		
< 2 months (n = 122)	21 (17.2%)	28.2 (0.00)
3–6 months (n = 115)	21 (18.3%)	
7+ months (n = 109)	48 (44.0%)	
Currently deployed (n = 170)	39 (22.9%)	

Table A.5
Proportion of Contractors with Probable Depression

Characteristic	Number (%)	Chi-Square (p-value)
Specialty		
Training/advising (n = 125)	24 (19.2%)	12.4 (0.05)
Land security (n = 188)	28 (14.9%)	
Maritime security (n = 51)	6 (11.8%)	
Transportation (n = 22)	7 (31.8%)	
Base support (n = 37)	13 (35.1%)	
Logistics/maintenance (n = 21)	4 (19.1%)	
Management (n = 28)	3 (10.7%)	
Other (n = 46)	8 (17.4%)	

Table A.5—Continued

Characteristic	Number (%)	Chi-Square (p-value)
Contract funder		
DoD (n = 169)	38 (22.5%)	6.24 (0.04)
DoS (n = 122)	25 (20.5%)	
Other (n = 226)	30 (13.3%)	
Citizenship		
United States (n = 300)	70 (23.3%)	12.48 (0.00)
United Kingdom (n = 120)	11 (9.2%)	
Other (n = 71)	10 (14.1%)	
Age		
Under 40 (n = 170)	28 (16.5%)	0.46 (0.50)
40 or older (n = 338)	64 (18.9%)	
Previous military experience		
Yes (n = 437)	72 (16.5%)	4.4 (0.04)
No (n = 80)	21 (26.3%)	
Carried a weapon as part of job		
Yes (n = 341)	53 (15.5%)	5.00 (0.03)
No (n = 169)	40 (23.7%)	
Number of deployments on contract		
1 (n = 105)	19 (18.1%)	1.16 (0.56)
2 (n = 77)	17 (22.1%)	
3 or more (n = 332)	56 (16.9%)	
Length of most recent contract		
< 2 months (n = 121)	14 (11.6%)	12.3 (0.01)
3–6 months (n = 116)	17 (14.7%)	
7+ months (n = 109)	31 (28.4%)	
Currently deployed (n = 170)	31 (18.2%)	

APPENDIX B

Sensitivity Analyses

The following tables show results using imputed data side by side with analyses conducted using raw data (reported earlier in this report). With the exception of a few cases, imputed results are very similar to those of the analyses conducted with raw data. In the few instances in which imputed results differ, the findings using raw data indicate marginal statistical significance and the analyses using the imputed data introduce enough uncertainty that tests for differences are no longer marginally statistically significant. We note where this has occurred. For the vast majority of analyses, however, imputed results reflect what we found in our analyses of raw data and provide confidence bands around estimates that take into account missing data.

Table B.1
Sensitivity Analysis Results: Contractor Deployment Experiences, Overall

		Raw Data	Imputed
Characteristic	**Number**	**Mean (std)/%**	**Mean/% (95% CI)**
DRRI: (perception of preparation for deployment) (higher score = more prepared; range: 0–12)	580	7.06 (3.43)	6.78 (6.50–7.06)
DRRI: combat exposure (higher score = more exposure; range: 0–24)	559	4.92 (5.52)	5.50 (5.06–5.94)
DRRI: living conditions (higher score = better living conditions; range: 0–17)	539	12.13 (3.32)	11.68 (11.4–12.0)
Carried a weapon as part of job	606	66.5%	65.4% (61.6%–69.2%)
Prior military experience	646	83.9%	83.5% (80.7%–86.4%)
Length of most recent deployment	617		
< 2 months	152	24.6%	24.9% (21.3%–28.3%)
3–6 months	143	23.2%	23.3% (17.5%–26.8%)
7+ months	126	20.4%	20.4% (17.2%–23.5%)
Currently deployed	196	31.8%	31.4% (27.5%–35.2%)
Number of deployments on contract with company	617		
1	123	19.9%	20.1% (16.9%–23.3%)
2	93	15.1%	15.0% (14.4%–17.8%)
3 or more	401	65.0%	64.9% (61.1%–68.7%)

Table B.2
Sensitivity Analysis Results: Individual DRRI Deployment Preparation Items

	Raw Data	Imputed
DRRI Preparation Item	**% in Agreement**	**% in Agreement (95% CI)**
I was informed about the role my unit was expected to play in the deployment. (n = 572)	76.9	73.7 (69.5–77.9)
When I was deployed I had a pretty good idea of how long the mission would take to complete. (n = 571)	76.5	73.3 (69.1–77.7)
I was adequately trained to work the shifts required of me during my deployment. (n = 572)	71.3	68.8 (64.4–73.1)
The equipment I was given functioned the way it was supposed to. (n = 577)	70.4	66.9 (62.9–70.8)
I received adequate training on how to use my equipment. (n = 573)	68.0	66.5 (62.5–70.5)
I had all the supplies and equipment needed to get my job done. (n = 580)	66.6	63.3 (59.1–67.4)
When I was deployed I felt I had adequate administrative/logistical support for travel and mission requirements. (n = 574)	61.7	58.8 (54.4–63.1)
I was accurately informed of what daily life would be like during my deployment. (n = 573)	61.3	59.3 (54.8–63.8)
When I was deployed I felt that I had been prepared with adequate, accurate intelligence to support my mission. (n = 573)	54.3	50.8 (46.1–55.5)
I saw as much combat as I expected. (n = 570)	50.5	50.4 (46.0–54.8)
When I was deployed I had access to adequate resources to help with stress. (n = 574)	25.6	24.1 (20.7–27.5)
My contracting company provided me with adequate stress management training. (n = 573)	23.6	22.2 (18.9–25.6)

Table B.3
Sensitivity Analysis Results: Reported Levels of Preparation for Deployment on Contract

	Raw Data		Imputed
Characteristic	Mean Score	Overall F-test or T-Test (p-value)	Mean Score (95% CI)
Specialty			
Training/advising (n = 135)	6.88	3.19 (0.00)	6.65 (6.07–7.22)
Land security (n = 220)	7.20		6.92 (6.50–7.35)
Maritime security (n = 58)	8.21		8.01 (7.13–8.88)
Transportation (n = 24)	5.45		5.42 (3.72–7.11)
Base support (n = 45)	5.95		5.81 (4.92–6.68)
Logistics/maintenance (n = 24)	8.17		7.82 (6.66–8.98)
Management (n = 37)	7.66		7.15 (6.09–8.20)
Other (n = 66)	6.43		5.97 (5.17–6.76)
Contract funder			
DoD (n = 186)	6.82	3.11 (0.05)[a]	6.69 (6.21–7.18)
DoS (n = 131)	6.63		6.43 (5.88–6.99)
Other (n = 263)	7.44		6.70 (4.89–8.50)
Citizenship			
United States (n = 300)	6.66	7.50 (0.00)	6.44 (6.09–6.80)
United Kingdom (n = 119)	7.24		7.00 (6.42–7.57)
Other (n = 71)	8.37		7.75 (7.06–8.43)
Age			
Under 40 (n = 170)	7.17	0.66 (0.51)	6.88 (6.40–7.37)
40 or older (n = 337)	6.96		6.73 (6.39–7.07)
Carried a weapon as part of job			
Yes (n = 379)	7.29	2.44 (0.02)	7.03 (6.69–7.37)
No (n = 192)	6.55		6.31 (5.87–6.76)
Previous military experience			
Yes (n = 488)	7.10	0.80 (0.42)	6.85 (6.55–7.15)
No (n = 91)	6.79		6.42 (5.78–7.06)

Table B.3—Continued

Characteristic	Raw Data: Mean Score	Raw Data: Overall F-test or T-Test (p-value)	Imputed: Mean Score (95% CI)
Length of most recent contract			
< 2 months (n = 140)	7.87	3.84 (0.01)	7.43 (6.88–7.99)
3–6 months (n = 129)	6.98		6.62 (6.07–7.17)
7+ months (n = 120)	6.72		6.53 (5.92–7.13)
Currently deployed (n = 189)	6.68		6.55 (6.05–7.05)
Number of deployments on contract			
1 (n = 117)	6.51	6.63 (0.00)	6.19 (5.62–6.76)
2 (n = 86)	6.22		6.06 (5.36–6.77)
3 or more (n = 373)	7.45		7.13 (6.80–7.46)

[a] Not significant with imputed data.

Table B.4
Sensitivity Analysis Results: Individual DRRI Combat Exposure Items

DRRI Combat Exposure Item	Raw Data: % of Respondents with Any Exposure	Imputed: % of Respondents with Any Exposure (95% CI)
I or members of my team encountered land or water mines and/or booby traps. (n = 553)	36.2	40.4 (36.2–44.6)
I or members of my team received hostile incoming fire from small arms, artillery, rockets, mortars, or bombs. (n = 554)	72.7	74.3 (70.4–78.2)
I was in a vehicle (for example, a truck, tank, armored personnel carrier, helicopter, plane, or boat) that was under fire. (n = 548)	39.4	45.3 (41.1–49.6)
I or members of my team were attacked by terrorists or civilians. (n = 553)	47.4	51.3 (47.1–55.6)
My team suffered casualties. (n = 549)	34.1	36.0 (31.8–40.2)
I personally witnessed someone from my team or an ally unit being seriously wounded or killed. (n = 554)	36.3	38.4 (33.8–43.1)

Table B.5
Sensitivity Analysis Results: Reported Levels of Combat Exposure During Deployment on Contract

	Raw Data		Imputed
Characteristic	**Mean Score**	**Overall F-Test (p-value)**	**Mean Score (95% CI)**
Specialty			
Training/advising (n = 149)	5.41	3.20 (0.00)	5.80 (4.89–6.70)
Land security (n = 251)	5.02		5.61 (4.89–6.33)
Maritime security (n = 63)	3.05		3.96 (2.64–5.29)
Transportation (n = 25)	8.78		8.84 (6.11–11.6)
Base support (n = 45)	4.27		4.77 (3.38–6.15)
Logistics/maintenance (n = 24)	3.02		3.68 (2.36–4.99)
Management (n = 37)	5.26		6.02 (4.09–7.95)
Other (n = 66)	4.50		5.51 (4.31–6.71)
Contract funder			
DoD (n = 184)	5.56	2.27 (0.10)	5.95 (5.19–6.70)
DoS (n = 129)	4.29		4.71 (3.88–5.55)
Other (n = 246)	4.76		5.57 (4.90–6.23)
Citizenship			
United States (n = 299)	5.52	5.29 (0.01)	6.00 (5.45–6.56)
United Kingdom (n = 113)	3.90		4.80 (3.90–5.69)
Other (n = 71)	3.80		4.70 (3.61–5.80)
Age			
Under 40 (n = 167)	5.50	1.01 (0.92)	5.49 (4.76–6.23)
40 or older (n = 333)	5.47		5.51 (4.96–6.05)
Carried a weapon as part of job			
Yes (n = 367)	5.10	1.03 (0.30)	5.61 (5.07–6.15)
No (n = 184)	4.59		5.29 (4.57–6.03)
Previous military experience			
Yes (n = 470)	5.06	1.42 (0.16)	5.58 (5.10–6.07)
No (n = 88)	4.26		5.06 (4.10–6.09)

Table B.5—Continued

Characteristic	Raw Data: Mean Score	Raw Data: Overall F-Test (p-value)	Imputed: Mean Score (95% CI)
Length of most recent contract			
< 2 months	3.35	11.67 (0.00)	4.37 (3.41–5.33)
3–6 months	5.29		5.85 (5.04–6.66)
7+ months	7.19		7.41 (6.41–8.41)
Currently deployed	4.35		4.89 (4.18–5.61)
Number of deployments on contract			
1 (n = 112)	4.29	1.05 (0.35)	4.94 (4.09–5.79)
2 (n = 84)	5.40		5.89 (4.74–7.05)
3 or more (n = 359)	4.97		5.59 (5.03–6.14)

Table B.6
Sensitivity Analysis Results: Individual DRRI Living Conditions Items, Positively Coded

DRRI Living Conditions Item (+)	Raw Data: Mean Score	Imputed: Mean Score (95% CI)
I had access to clean clothing when I needed it. (n = 539)	4.5	4.4 (4.3–4.5)
I could get a cold drink (for example, water, or juice) when I wanted one. (n = 536)	4.4	4.3 (4.2–4.4)
I had access to bathrooms or showers when I needed them. (n = 538)	4.3	4.2 (4.1–4.3)
I got as much sleep as I needed. (n = 539)	3.4	3.4 (3.3–3.5)
I was able to get enough privacy. (n = 539)	3.4	3.2 (3.1–3.4)
I got the R&R (rest and relaxation) that I needed. (n = 535)	3.4	3.3 (3.2–3.4)
I received my mail in a timely manner. (n = 531)	3.1	3.0 (2.9–3.2)
I had access to phone/Internet for managing personal business (for example, to pay bills) and for maintaining contact with family/friends. (n = 538)	3.9	3.8 (3.7–4.0)
I had the equipment or supplies to do what I needed to do. (n = 530)	3.8	3.7 (3.6–3.9)
I felt comfortable living in the culture or cultures where I was deployed. (n = 538)	3.8	3.7 (3.6–3.8)

Table B.7
Sensitivity Analysis Results: Individual DRRI Living Conditions Items, Reverse-Coded

	Raw Data	Imputed
DRRI Living Conditions Item (–)	**Mean Score**	**Mean Score (95% CI)**
The food I had to eat was of very poor quality (for example, bad or old MREs). (n = 539)	2.1	2.2 (2.0–2.3)
The conditions I lived in were extremely unsanitary. (n = 537)	2.0	2.1 (2.0–2.2)
The living space was too crowded. (n = 537)	2.6	2.7 (2.5–2.9)
The workdays were too long. (n = 537)	2.9	2.9 (2.8–3.1)
I was subjected to loud noises. (n = 537)	3.3	3.2 (3.1–3.4)
My daily activities were restricted because of local religious or ethnic customs. (n = 536)	2.4	2.6 (2.5–2.7)
I felt pressure to conform to the local culture, making it difficult for me to do my job. (n = 538)	1.9	2.0 (1.9–2.2)

Table B.8
Sensitivity Analysis Results: Living Conditions

	Raw Data		Imputed
Characteristic	**Mean Score**	**Overall F-Test (p-value)**	**Mean Score (95% CI)**
Specialty			
Training/advising (n = 127)	11.87	1.63 (0.12)	11.48 (10.88–12.09)
Land security (n = 202)	12.31		11.78 (11.29–12.26)
Maritime security (n = 53)	12.95		12.45 (11.63–13.26)
Transportation (n = 22)	10.36		10.22 (8.83–11.59)
Base support (n = 39)	12.10		11.86 (11.04–12.68)
Logistics/maintenance (n = 21)	12.52		12.25 (11.08–13.43)
Management (n = 28)	12.06		11.56 (10.20–12.91)
Other (n = 47)	11.92		11.32 (10.59–12.06)
Contract funder			
DoD (n = 175)	11.8	3.21 (0.04)[a]	11.42 (10.94–11.90)
DoS (n = 124)	11.8		11.55 (10.94–12.16)
Other (n = 239)	12.5		11.92 (11.47–12.37)

Table B.8—Continued

Characteristic	Raw Data: Mean Score	Raw Data: Overall F-Test (p-value)	Imputed: Mean Score (95% CI)
Citizenship			
United States (n = 300)	11.6	12.28 (0.00)	11.3 (10.9–11.7)
United Kingdom (n = 120)	12.9		12.3 (11.7–12.8)
Other (n = 70)	13.3		12.3 (11.6–13.1)
Age			
Under 40 (n = 170)	11.9	1.17 (0.22)	11.5 (11.0–12.0)
40 or older (n = 337)	12.3		11.8 (11.4–12.2)
Carried a weapon as part of job			
Yes (n = 357)	12.2	0.25 (0.80)	11.8 (11.8–12.1)
No (n = 174)	12.1		11.5 (11.1–12.0)
Previous military experience			
Yes (n = 542)	12.1	−0.18 (0.86)	11.7 (11.3–12.0)
No (n = 104)	12.2		11.6 (10.9–12.3)
Length of most recent contract			
< 2 months (n = 126)	13.1	5.90 (0.00)	12.4 (11.8–12.9)
3–6 months (n = 121)	11.8		11.3 (10.7–11.9)
7+ months (n = 113)	11.4		11.1 (10.5–11.7)
Currently deployed (n = 177)	12.2		11.8 (11.3–12.3)
Number of deployments on contract			
1 (n = 107)	12.1	1.86 (0.16)	11.6 (11.0–12.3)
2 (n = 82)	11.5		11.2 (10.4–11.9)
3 or more (n = 346)	12.3		11.8 (11.4–12.2)

[a] Not significant with imputed data

Table B.9
Sensitivity Analysis Results: Contractor Mental Health, Overall

	Raw Data		Imputed
Characteristic	**Number**	**%**	**% (95% CI)**
Probable PTSD	518	25	22 (18–25)
Depression	518	18	16 (13–20)
Alcohol misuse	529	47	44 (39–51)
High-risk drinking	529	10	8 (6–10)
Tobacco use	530	37	37 (33–41)

Table B.10
Sensitivity Analysis Results: Proportion of Contractors with Probable PTSD

	Raw Data		Imputed
Characteristic	**Number (%)**	**Chi-Square (p-value)**	**% (95% CI)**
Specialty			
Training/advising (n = 125)	39 (31.2)	24.3 (0.00)	28.1 (20.6–35.7)
Land security (n = 187)	42 (22.5)		19.0 (13.7–24.3)
Maritime security (n = 52)	2 (3.9)		3.5 (0.0–8.3)
Transportation (n = 22)	11 (50.0)		44.8 (24.6–65.0)
Base support (n = 37)	12 (32.4)		30.0 (16.2–43.8)
Logistics/maintenance (n = 21)	5 (23.8)		22.5 (4.9–40.1)
Management (n = 28)	6 (21.4)		19.7 (5.4–34.0)
Other (n = 46)	12 (26.1)		19.8 (10.0–29.9)
Contract funder			
DoD (n = 169)	54 (32.0)	10.8 (0.00)	28.2 (21.8–34.7)
DoS (n = 121)	34 (28.1)		26.2 (18.7–33.7)
Other (n = 227)	41 (18.1)		14.9 (10.7–19.2)
Citizenship			
United States (n = 299)	96 (32.1)	20.48 (0.00)	27.7 (23.0–32.5)
United Kingdom (n = 120)	15 (12.5)		10.5 (5.6–15.5)
Other (n = 71)	12 (16.9)		15.8 (7.3–24.4)

Table B.10—Continued

Characteristic	Raw Data: Number (%)	Raw Data: Chi-Square (p-value)	Imputed: % (95% CI)
Age			
Under 40 (n = 169)	42 (24.9)	0.01 (0.94)	21.9 (17.9–26.0)
40 or older (n = 338)	85 (25.2)		20.9 (14.9–26.7)
Previous military experience			
Yes (n = 437)	108 (24.7)	0.08 (0.77)	21.5 (17.8–25.2)
No (n = 80)	21 (26.3)		21.8 (13.8–29.8)
Carried a weapon as part of job			
Yes (n = 341)	78 (22.9)	2.7 (0.10)	20.2 (16.1–24.1)
No (n = 169)	50 (29.6)		24.3 (18.3–30.3)
Number of deployments on contract			
1 (n = 105)	25 (23.8)	3.82 (0.15)	20.7 (13.5–27.9)
2 (n = 77)	26 (33.8)		28.0 (18.7–37.2)
3 or more (n = 332)	77 (23.2)		20.4 (16.2–24.5)
Length of most recent contract			
< 2 months (n = 122)	21 (17.2)	28.2 (0.00)	14.7 (8.6–20.7)
3–6 months (n = 115)	21 (18.3)		16.8 (9.8–23.8)
7+ months (n = 109)	48 (44.0)		37.6 (29.1–46.0)
Currently deployed (n = 170)	39 (22.9)		20.2 (14.4–26.0)

Table B.11
Sensitivity Analysis Results: Proportion of Contractors with Probable Depression

Characteristic	Raw Data		Imputed
	Number (%)	Chi-Square (p-value)	% (95% CI)
Specialty			
Training/advising (n = 125)	24 (19.2%)	12.4 (0.05)	17.7 (11.1–24.3)
Land security (n = 188)	28 (14.9%)		13.1 (8.5–17.7)
Maritime security (n = 51)	6 (11.8%)		9.7 (2.3–17.1)
Transportation (n = 22)	7 (31.8%)		28.4 (10.2–46.6)
Base support (n = 37)	13 (35.1%)		33.1 (18.8–47.4)
Logistics/maintenance (n = 21)	4 (19.1%)		17.5 (8.1–15.7)
Management (n = 28)	3 (10.7%)		16.2 (2.8–29.6)
Other (n = 46)	8 (17.4%)		15.0 (4.7–25.3)
Contract funder			
DoD (n = 169)	38 (22.5%)	6.24 (0.04)	20.6 (14.2–26.9)
DoS (n = 122)	25 (20.5%)		19.0 (12.3–25.6)
Other (n = 226)	30 (13.3%)		12.1 (8.0–16.2)
Citizenship			
United States (n = 300)	70 (23.3%)	12.48 (0.00)	20.2 (15.8–24.8)
United Kingdom (n = 120)	11 (9.2%)		8.7 (4.0–13.4)
Other (n = 71)	10 (14.1%)		13.1 (5.9–20.4)
Age			
Under 40 (n = 170)	28 (16.5%)	0.46 (0.50)	14.6 (9.4–19.7)
40 or older (n = 338)	64 (18.9%)		17.2 (13.2–21.1)
Previous military experience			
Yes (n = 437)	72 (16.5%)	4.4 (0.04)	15.1 (11.7–18.5)
No (n = 80)	21 (26.3%)		22.3 (13.9–30.6)
Carried a weapon as part of job			
Yes (n = 341)	53 (15.5%)	5.00 (0.03)	14.0 (10.4–17.6)
No (n = 169)	40 (23.7%)		20.6 (14.8–26.3)

Table B.11—Continued

Characteristic	Raw Data		Imputed
	Number (%)	Chi-Square (p-value)	% (95% CI)
Number of deployments on contract			
1 (n = 105)	19 (18.1%)	1.16 (0.56)	16.9 (9.5–24.2)
2 (n = 77)	17 (22.1%)		19.2 (10.7–27.6)
3 or more (n = 332)	56 (16.9%)		15.4 (11.7–19.2)
Length of most recent contract			
< 2 months (n = 121)	14 (11.6%)	12.3 (0.01)	11.4 (5.3–17.5)
3–6 months (n = 116)	17 (14.7%)		12.5 (6.9–18.0)
7+ months (n = 109)	31 (28.4%)		25.4 (17.4–33.5)
Currently deployed (n = 170)	31 (18.2%)		17.0 (11.6–22.5)

Table B.12
Sensitivity Analysis Results: Overall Health and Other Health Conditions as a Result of Deployment

		Raw Data	Imputed
Overall Health (n = 535)	**Number**	**%**	**% (95% CI)**
Excellent	159	30	27 (23–31)
Very good	207	39	41 (37–46)
Good	113	21	22 (18–25)
Fair	41	8	7 (5–10)
Poor	15	3	3 (1–4)

Table B.13
Sensitivity Analysis Results: Other Health Conditions as a Result of Deployment (not including PTSD-only responses)

	Raw Data		Imputed
Characteristic	Number with Other Condition (%)	Chi-Square (p-value)	% with Other Condition (95% CI)
Overall (n = 534)	208 (39.0%)		37.8 (33.4–42.1)
Specialty			
Training/advising (n = 127)	54 (42.5%)	17.6 (0.01)	40.1 (31.7–48.5)
Land security (n = 198)	80 (40.4%)		39.4 (31.9–46.9)
Maritime security (n = 53)	8 (15.1%)		14.8 (4.7–24.8)
Transportation (n = 22)	12 (54.6%)		52.4 (31.1–73.6)
Base support (n = 38)	15 (39.5%)		42.0 (25.5–58.5)
Logistics/maintenance (n = 21)	8 (38.1%)		33.8 (14.2–53.3)
Management (n = 28)	9 (32.1%)		34.6 (15.7–53.5)
Other (n = 47)	22 (46.8%)		42.9 (28.2–57.6)
Contract funder			
DoD (n = 175)	81 (46.3%)	13.4 (0.00)	45.2 (38.1–52.4)
DoS (n = 121)	55 (45.5%)		44.7 (35.4–53.9)
Other (n = 237)	72 (30.4%)		29.5 (23.9–35.1)
Citizenship			
United States (n = 299)	157 (52.5%)	56.5 (0.00)	48.3% (42.2%–54.3%)
United Kingdom (n = 120)	19 (15.8%)		18.2% (11.9%–24.5%)
Other (n = 71)	17 (23.9%)		29.2% (19.7%–38.6%)

Table B.14
Sensitivity Analysis Results: Average Combat Exposure Ratings for Those with and Without Other Health Conditions as a Result of Deployment (not including PTSD-only responses)

	Raw Data		Imputed
Other Health Condition	Average Combat Score	T-Test (P-Value)	Average Combat Score (95% CI)
Yes (n = 215)	6.70	6.6 (0.00)	6.94 (6.19–7.70)
No (n = 310)	3.62		4.63 (4.10–5.16)

Table B.15
Sensitivity Analysis Results: Rates of Probable PTSD and Depression for Those with and Without Other Health Conditions as a Result of Deployment (not including PTSD-only responses)

	Raw Data		Imputed	
Characteristic	Number with Probable PTSD (%)	Number with Probable Depression (%)	% with Probable PTSD (95% CI)	% with Probable Depression (95% CI)
Listed other health condition	87 (43.1%)	61 (30.1%)	37 (31–44)	26 (21–33)
Did not list other health condition	42 (13.3%)	31 (9.9%)	12 (8–16)	10 (6–14)
Chi-square (p-value)	58.12 (0.00)	34.31 (0.00)		

Table B.16
Sensitivity Analysis Results: PTSD Status, by Access to Company-Provided Stress Management Resources

	Raw Data		Imputed
Characteristic	Number with Probable PTSD/ Total Number (%)	p-Value	% (95% CI)
Received adequate stress management training			
Yes	16/121 (13.2%)	< 0.01	11.9 (6.6–17.3)
No	111/391 (28.4%)		24.3 (20.3–28.4)
Had adequate resources to help with stress while deployed			
Yes	15/137 (11.0%)	< 0.01	10.7 (5.7–15.7)
No	114/376 (30.3%)		25.0 (20.9–29.2)
Company provides access to resources to help with postdeployment stress problems			
Yes	10/90 (11.1%)	< 0.01	10.5 (4.5–16.4)
No	117/425 (27.5%)		24.0 (20.1–27.8)

Table B.17
Sensitivity Analysis Results: Depression Status, by Access to Company-Provided Stress Management Resources

	Raw Data		Imputed
Characteristic	Number with Probable MDD/ Total Number (%)	P-Value	% (95% CI)
Received adequate stress management training			
Yes	6/120 (5.0%)	< 0.01	5.3 (1.0–9.8)
No	86/392 (21.9%)		19.4 (15.5–23.3)
Had adequate resources to help with stress while deployed			
Yes	9/136 (6.6%)	< 0.01	7.0 (2.5–11.3)
No	84/377 (22.3%)		19.3 (15.2–23.3)
Company provides access to resources to help with postdeployment stress problems			
Yes	4/90 (4.4%)	< 0.01	4.9 (0.4–9.4)
No	88/426 (20.7%)		18.8 (15.0–22.5)

Table B.18
Sensitivity Analysis Results: Perceived Barriers to Mental Health Treatment

	Raw Data		Imputed	
	Number in Agreement/ Total Number (%)		% (95% CI)	
Response	Respondents with Probable PTSD or Depression (n = 159)	Respondents Without Probable PTSD or Depression (n = 360)	Respondents with Probable PTSD or Depression	Respondents Without Probable PTSD or Depression
I don't trust mental health professionals.	65/157 (41.4%)	73/352 (20.7%)	39 (31–46)	20 (15–25)
I don't know where to get help.	42/157 (26.8%)	32/349 (9.2%)	25 (18–32)	8 (5–12)
I don't have adequate transportation.	16/154 (10.4%)	15/351 (4.3%)	9 (5–14)	4 (2–6)
It is difficult to schedule an appointment.	41/157 (26.1%)	37/349 (10.6%)	25 (18–31)	10 (7–14)
There would be difficulty getting time off work for treatment.	42/157 (26.8%)	48/349 (13.8%)	26 (20–33)	15 (11–19)
Mental health care costs too much money.	78/157 (49.7%)	85/347 (24.5%)	47 (39–54)	24 (19–29)
It would be too embarrassing.	79/157 (50.3%)	97/349 (27.8%)	47 (41–56)	27 (23–32)
It would harm my career.	109/156 (69.9%)	171/350 (48.9%)	67 (59–75)	51 (46–56)
My colleagues might have less confidence in me.	107/157 (68.2%)	149/349 (42.7%)	66 (58–73)	45 (40–50)
My supervisor or other officials at my company might treat me differently.	111/156 (71.2%)	157/349 (45.0%)	68 (61–75)	47 (41–52)
My supervisor or other officials at my company would blame me for the problem.	69/157 (44.0%)	75/349 (21.5%)	41 (34–49)	21 (17–26)
I would be seen as weak.	103/155 (66.5%)	137/347 (39.5%)	64 (57–71)	40 (35–46)
Mental health care doesn't work.	28/157 (17.8%)	37/347 (10.7%)	17 (11–22)	11 (7–15)

References

"American Contractors in Iraq," homepage, undated. As of July 19, 2013: http://www.americancontractorsiniraq.com

American National Standards Institute and ASIS International, *Management System for Quality of Private Security Company Operations—Requirements with Guidance*, Alexandria, Va., ANSI/ASIS PSC.1-2012, 2012.

Atwoli, Lukoye, Dan J. Stein, David R. Williams, Katie A. Mclaughlin, Maria Petukhova, Ronald C. Kessler, and Karestan C. Koenen, "Trauma and Posttraumatic Stress Disorder in South Africa: Analysis from the South African Stress and Health Study," *BMC Psychiatry*, Vol. 13, No. 1, 2013, pp. 182–193.

Avant, Deborah D., *The Market for Force: The Consequences of Privatizing Security*, Cambridge, UK: Cambridge University Press, 2005.

Barlas, Frances M., William Bryan Higgins, Jacqueline C. Pflieger, and Kelly Diecker, *2011 Health Related Behaviors Survey of Active Duty Military Personnel*, Falls Church, Va.: U.S. Department of Defense, TRICARE Management Activity, Defense Health Cost Assessment and Program Evaluation, and U.S. Coast Guard, 2013. As of August 28, 2013: http://www.murray.senate.gov/public/_cache/files/889efd07-2475-40ee-b3b0-508947957a0f/final-2011-hrb-active-duty-survey-report.pdf

Bliese, Paul D., Kathleen M. Wright, Amy B. Adler, Jeffrey L. Thomas, and Charles W. Hoge, "Timing of Postcombat Mental Health Assessments," *Psychological Services*, Vol. 4, No. 3, July 2007, pp. 141–148.

Boscarino, Joseph A., Richard E. Adams, and Charles R. Figley, "Worker Productivity and Outpatient Service Use after the September 11th Attacks: Results from the New York City Terrorism Outcome Study," *American Journal of Industrial Medicine*, Vol. 49, No. 8, August 2006, pp. 670–682.

Bromet, Evelyn, Laura H. Andrade, Irving Hwang, Nancy A. Sampson, Jordi Alonso, Giovanni de Girolamo, Ron de Graaf, Koen Demyttenaere, Chiyi Hu, and Noboru Iwata, "Cross-National Epidemiology of Dsm-IV Major Depressive Episode," *BMC Medicine*, Vol. 9, No. 1, 2011, pp. 90–106.

Bronner, M. B., N. Peek, M. de Vries, A. E. Bronner, B. F. Last, and M. A. Grootenhuis, "A Community-Based Survey of Posttraumatic Stress Disorder in the Netherlands," *Journal of Traumatic Stress*, Vol. 22, No. 1, February 2009, pp. 74–78.

Browne, Tess, Amy Iversen, Lisa Hull, Lorna Workman, Christopher Barker, Oded Horn, Margaret Jones, Dominic Murphy, Neil Greenberg, and Roberto Rona, "How Do Experiences in Iraq Affect Alcohol Use among Male UK Armed Forces Personnel?" *Occupational and Environmental Medicine*, Vol. 65, No. 9, September 2008, pp. 628–633.

Buckman, Joshua E. J., Josefin Sundin, Talya Greene, Nicola T. Fear, Christopher Dandeker, Neil Greenberg, and Simon Wessely, "The Impact of Deployment Length on the Health and Well-Being of Military Personnel: A Systematic Review of the Literature," *Occupational and Environmental Medicine*, Vol. 68, No. 1, January 2011, pp. 69–76.

Bush, Kristen, Daniel R. Kivlahan, Mary B. McDonell, Stephan D. Fihn, and Katharine A. Bradley, "The AUDIT Alcohol Consumption Questions (AUDIT-C): An Effective Brief Screening Test for Problem Drinking," *Archives of Internal Medicine*, Vol. 158, No. 16, September 14, 1998, pp. 1789–1795.

Chapman, Paula L., David Cabrera, Christina Varela-Mayer, Monty Baker, Christine Elnitsky, Charles Figley, Ryan M. Thurman, Chii-Dean Lin, and Paul Mayer, "Training, Deployment Preparation, and Combat Experiences of Deployed Health Care Personnel: Key Findings from Deployed US Army Combat Medics Assigned to Line Units," *Military Medicine*, Vol. 177, No. 3, March 2012, pp. 270–277.

Chesterman, Simon, "Lawyers, Guns, and Money: The Governance of Business Activities in Conflict Zones," *Chicago Journal of International Law*, Vol. 11, No. 2, Winter 2010–2011, pp. 321–341.

Clark, Kenneth A., *Other Sons and Daughters: A True Account of Civilian Convoy Drivers in Iraq*, Stahlstown, Pa.: Silverbear Graphics, 2012.

Collins, Rebecca L., Eunice C. Wong, Jennifer L. Cerully, Dana Schultz, and Nicole K. Eberhart, *Interventions to Reduce Mental Health Stigma and Discrimination: A Literature Review to Guide Evaluation of California's Mental Health Prevention and Early Intervention Initiative*, Santa Monica, Calif.: RAND Corporation, TR-1318-CMHSA, 2012. As of August 27, 2013: http://www.rand.org/pubs/technical_reports/TR1318.html

Commission on Army Acquisition and Program Management in Expeditionary Operations, *Urgent Reform Required: Army Expeditionary Contracting*, Washington, D.C., October 31, 2007. As of July 19, 2013:
http://www.army.mil/docs/Gansler_Commission_Report_Final_071031.pdf

Cotton, Sarah K., Ulrich Petersohn, Molly Dunigan, Q Burkhart, Megan Zander-Cotugno, Edward O'Connell, and Michael Webber, *Hired Guns: Views About Armed Security Contractors in Operation Iraqi Freedom*, Santa Monica, Calif.: RAND Corporation, MG-987-SRF, 2010. As of July 19, 2013: http://www.rand.org/pubs/monographs/MG987.html

Creamer, Mark, Philip Burgess, and Alexander Cowell McFarlane, "Post-Traumatic Stress Disorder: Findings from the Australian National Survey of Mental Health and Well-Being," *Psychological Medicine*, Vol. 31, No. 7, 2001, pp. 1237–1247.

Crisp, Arthur, Michael Gelder, Eileen Goddard, and Howard Meltzer, "Stigmatization of People with Mental Illnesses: A Follow-Up Study Within the Changing Minds Campaign of the Royal College of Psychiatrists," *World Psychiatry*, Vol. 4, No. 2, June 2005, pp. 106–113.

Dalesto, Emery P., "Blackwater Suit Ends 7 Years after Fallujah Deaths," *Boston Globe*, 2012. As of July 10, 2013:
http://www.boston.com/news/nation/articles/2012/01/06/
blackwater_suit_ends_7_years_after_fallujah_deaths

DoD—*See* U.S. Department of Defense.

Drummond, Katie, "Combat 'Burn Pits' Ruin Immune System, Study Shows," *Wired*, May 23, 2012. As of July 19, 2013:
http://www.wired.com/dangerroom/2012/05/burn-pits

Dunigan, Molly, *Victory for Hire: Private Security Companies' Impact on Military Effectiveness*, Stanford, Calif.: Stanford University Press, 2011.

Engelhard, Iris M., Marcel A. Van Den Hout, Jos Weerts, Arnoud Arntz, Joop J. C. M. Hox, and Richard J. McNally, "Deployment-Related Stress and Trauma in Dutch Soldiers Returning from Iraq Prospective Study," *British Journal of Psychiatry*, Vol. 191, No. 2, August 2007, pp. 140–145.

Evans-Lacko, Sara, Claire Henderson, and Graham Thornicroft, "Public Knowledge, Attitudes and Behaviour Regarding People with Mental Illness in England 2009–2012," *British Journal of Psychiatry*, Vol. 202, No. 55 (supplement), 2013, pp. s51–s57.

Evans-Lacko, Sara, Estelle Malcolm, Keon West, Diana Rose, Jillian London, Nicolas Rüsch, Kirsty Little, Claire Henderson, and Graham Thornicroft, "Influence of Time to Change's Social Marketing Interventions on Stigma in England 2009–2011," *British Journal of Psychiatry*, Vol. 202, No. s55, 2013, pp. s77–s88.

Fainaru, Steve, *Big Boy Rules: America's Mercenaries Fighting in Iraq*, Philadelphia, Pa.: Da Capo Press, 2008.

Fear, Nicola T., Amy Iversen, Howard Meltzer, Lorna Workman, Lisa Hull, Neil Greenberg, Christopher Barker, Tess Browne, Mark Earnshaw, Oded Horn, Margaret Jones, Dominic Murphy, Roberto J. Rona, Matthew Hotopf, and Simon Wessely, "Patterns of Drinking in the UK Armed Forces," *Addiction*, Vol. 102, No. 11, 2007, pp. 1749–1759.

Fear, Nicola T., Margaret Jones, Dominic Murphy, Lisa Hull, Amy C. Iversen, Bolaji Coker, Louise Machell, Josefin Sundin, Charlotte Woodhead, Norman Jones, Neil Greenberg, Sabine Landau, Christopher Dandeker, Roberto J. Rona, Matthew Hotopf, and Simon Wessely, "What Are the Consequences of Deployment to Iraq and Afghanistan on the Mental Health of the UK Armed Forces? A Cohort Study," *The Lancet*, Vol. 375, No. 9728, May 22, 2010, pp. 1783–1797.

Feinstein, Anthony, and Maggie Botes, "The Psychological Health of Contractors Working in War Zones," *Journal of Traumatic Stress*, Vol. 22, No. 2, April 2009, pp. 102–105.

Geraghty, Tony, *Guns for Hire: The Inside Story of Freelance Soldiering*, London: Piatkus Books, 2008.

Gettleman, Jeffrey, "Enraged Mob in Fallujah Kills 4 American Contractors," *New York Times*, March 31, 2004. As of July 19, 2013:
http://www.nytimes.com/2004/03/31/international/worldspecial/31CND-IRAQ.html

Gould, Matthew, Amy Adler, Mark Zamorski, Carl Castro, Natalie Hanily, Nicole Steele, Steve Kearney, and Neil Greenberg, "Do Stigma and Other Perceived Barriers to Mental Health Care Differ across Armed Forces?" *Journal of the Royal Society of Medicine*, Vol. 103, No. 4, 2010, pp. 148–156.

Gould, Matthew, Neil Greenberg, and Jacquie Hetherton, "Stigma and the Military: Evaluation of a PTSD Psychoeducational Program," *Journal of Traumatic Stress*, Vol. 20, No. 4, 2007, pp. 505–515.

Greenberg, Neil, "The Mental Health of Security Contractors Cannot Be Ignored," *Huffington Post*, January 10, 2012. As of July 19, 2013:
http://www.huffingtonpost.co.uk/professor-neil-greenberg/danny-fitzsimons-mental-health-g4s-_b_1929016.html

"Halliburton Hit Hard by Iraq Kidnappings," Associated Press, April 14, 2004. As of July 19, 2013:
http://www.foxnews.com/story/0,2933,117046,00.html

Hoge, Charles W., Jennifer L. Auchterlonie, and Charles S. Milliken, "Mental Health Problems, Use of Mental Health Services, and Attrition from Military Service After Returning from Deployment to Iraq or Afghanistan," *Journal of the American Medical Association*, Vol. 295, No. 9, March 1, 2006, pp. 1023–1032.

Hoge, Charles W., and Carl A. Castro, "Impact of Combat Duty in Iraq and Afghanistan on the Mental Health of U.S. Soldiers: Findings from the Walter Reed Army Institute of Research Land Combat Study," *Strategies to Maintain Combat Readiness During Extended Deployments: A Human Systems Approach*, papers presented at the RTO Human Factors and Medicine Panel Symposium, Prague, Czech Republic: NATO Research and Technology Organisation, 2005, pp. 11-11–11-16. As of July 19, 2013:
http://ftp.rta.nato.int/public/PubFullText/RTO/MP/RTO-MP-HFM-124/MP-HFM-124-11.pdf

Hoge, Charles W., Carl A. Castro, Steven C. Messer, Dennis McGurk, Dave I. Cotting, and Robert L. Koffman, "Combat Duty in Iraq and Afghanistan, Mental Health Problems, and Barriers to Care," *New England Journal of Medicine*, Vol. 351, No. 1, July 1, 2004, pp. 13–22.

Hoge, Charles W., Dennis McGurk, Jeffrey L. Thomas, Anthony L. Cox, Charles C. Engel, and Carl A. Castro, "Mild Traumatic Brain Injury in US Soldiers Returning from Iraq," *New England Journal of Medicine*, Vol. 358, No. 5, 2008, pp. 453–463.

Holowka, Darren W., and Brian P. Marx, "Assessing PTSD-Related Functional Impairment and Quality of Life," in Beck, J. Gayle and Denise M. Sloan, eds., *The Oxford Handbook of Traumatic Stress Disorders*, New York: Oxford University Press, 2012, pp. 315–330.

Hotopf, Matthew, Lisa Hull, Nicola T. Fear, Tess Browne, Oded Horn, Amy Iversen, Margaret Jones, Dominic Murphy, Duncan Bland, and Mark Earnshaw, "The Health of UK Military Personnel Who Deployed to the 2003 Iraq War: A Cohort Study," *The Lancet*, Vol. 367, No. 9524, 2006, pp. 1731–1741.

Institute of Medicine, *Returning Home from Iraq and Afghanistan: Assessment of Readjustment Needs of Veterans, Service Members, and Their Families*, Washington, D.C.: National Academies Press, 2013.

"International Code of Conduct for Private Security Service Providers," 2010. As of August 1, 2013:
http://www.eda.admin.ch/etc/medialib/downloads/edazen/topics/intla.Par.0001.File.tmp/INTERNATIONAL%20CODE%20OF%20CONDUCT%20dtc.pdf

Isenberg, David, *Shadow Force: Private Security Contractors in Iraq*, Westport, Conn.: Praeger Security International, 2008.

Iversen, Amy C., Lauren van Staden, Jamie Hacker Hughes, Tess Browne, Lisa Hull, John Hall, Neil Greenberg, Roberto J. Rona, Matthew Hotopf, Simon Wessely, and Nicola T. Fear, "The Prevalence of Common Mental Disorders and PTSD in the UK Military: Using Data from a Clinical Interview-Based Study," *BMC Psychiatry*, Vol. 9, No. 1, January 2009, pp. 68–79.

Iversen, Amy C., Lauren van Staden, Jamie H. Hughes, Neil Greenberg, Matthew Hotopf, Roberto J. Rona, Graham Thornicroft, Simon Wessely, and Nicola T. Fear, "The Stigma of Mental Health Problems and Other Barriers to Care in the UK Armed Forces," *BMC Health Services Research*, Vol. 11, No. 1, 2011, pp. 31–40.

Jakupcak, Matthew, Jane Luterek, Stephen Hunt, Daniel Conybeare, and Miles McFall, "Posttraumatic Stress and Its Relationship to Physical Health Functioning in a Sample of Iraq and Afghanistan War Veterans Seeking Postdeployment VA Health Care," *Journal of Nervous and Mental Disease*, Vol. 196, No. 5, 2008, pp. 425–428.

Joint Mental Health Advisory Team 7, "Operation Enduring Freedom 2010 Afghanistan," 2011. As of August 28, 2013:
http://www.armymedicine.army.mil/reports/mhat/mhat_vii/J_MHAT_7.pdf

Jorm, Anthony F., "Mental Health Literacy Public Knowledge and Beliefs About Mental Disorders," *British Journal of Psychiatry*, Vol. 177, No. 5, 2000, pp. 396–401.

Kelly, Suzanne, "Confessions of a Private Security Contractor," CNN, December 27, 2011. As of July 19, 2013:
http://security.blogs.cnn.com/2011/12/27/confessions-of-a-private-security-contractor

Kessler, Ronald C., Shanyang Zhao, Steven J. Katz, Anthony C. Kouzis, Richard G. Frank, Mark Edlund, and Philip Leaf, "Past-Year Use of Outpatient Services for Psychiatric Problems in the National Comorbidity Survey," *American Journal of Psychiatry*, Vol. 156, No. 1, 1999, pp. 115–123.

King, Lynda A., Daniel W. King, Dawne S. Vogt, Jeffrey Knight, and Rita E. Samper, "Deployment Risk and Resilience Inventory: A Collection of Measures for Studying Deployment-Related Experiences of Military Personnel and Veterans," *Military Psychology*, Vol. 18, No. 2, 2006, pp. 89–120.

Kinsey, Christopher, *Corporate Soldiers and International Security: The Rise of Private Military Companies*, London: Routledge, 2006.

Knickerbocker, Brad, "Silent Surge in Contractor 'Armies,'" *Christian Science Monitor*, July 18, 2007. As of July 19, 2013:
http://www.csmonitor.com/2007/0718/p01s02-usmi.html

Krahmann, Elke, *States, Citizens and the Privatisation of Security*, New York: Cambridge University Press, 2010.

Löwe, Bernd, Kurt Kroenke, and Kerstin Gräfe, "Detecting and Monitoring Depression with a Two-Item Questionnaire (PHQ-2)," *Journal of Psychosomatic Research*, Vol. 58, No. 2, February 2005, pp. 163–171.

MacManus, Deirdre, Kimberlie Dean, M. Al Bakir, A. C. Iversen, L. Hull, T. Fahy, S. Wessely, and N. T. Fear, "Violent Behaviour in UK Military Personnel Returning Home After Deployment," *Psychological Medicine*, Vol. 42, No. 8, 2012, pp. 1663–1673.

MacManus, Deirdre, Kimberlie Dean, Margaret Jones, Roberto J. Rona, Neil Greenberg, Lisa Hull, Tom Fahy, Simon Wessely, and Nicola T. Fear, "Violent Offending by UK Military Personnel Deployed to Iraq and Afghanistan: A Data Linkage Cohort Study," *The Lancet*, Vol. 381, No. 9870, March 16, 2013, pp. 907–917.

March on Stress, homepage, undated. As of September 25, 2013:
http://marchonstress.com/march-on-stress

Messenger, Katy, Lorna Farquharson, Pippa Stallworthy, Paul Cawkill, and Neil Greenberg, "The Experiences of Security Industry Contractors Working in Iraq: An Interpretative Phenomenological Analysis," *Journal of Occupational and Environmental Medicine*, Vol. 54, No. 7, July 2012, pp. 859–867.

Miller, T. Christian, "AIG Faces Inquiry over Medical Care for U.S. Contractors," *ProPublica*, April 22, 2009a. As of July 31, 2013:
http://www.propublica.org/article/aig-faces-inquiry-over-medical-care-for-u.s.-contractors-422

———, "Congressional Hearing: Officials Admit Major Flaws in Program to Aid Wounded War-Zone Workers," *ProPublica*, June 19, 2009b. As of July 31, 2013:
http://www.propublica.org/article/congressional-hearing-officials-acknowledge-program-to-treat-war-contra-619

———, "Foreign Workers for U.S. Are Casualties Twice Over," *ProPublica*, June 19, 2009c. As of July 13, 2013:
http://www.propublica.org/article/foreign-workers-for-u.s.-are-casualties-twice-over-619

———, "The Other Victims of Battlefield Stress; Defense Contractors' Mental Health Neglected," *ProPublica*, February 26, 2010a. As of July 31, 2013:
http://www.propublica.org/article/injured-contractors-the-other-victims-of-battlefield-stress-224

———, "This Year, Contractor Deaths Exceed Military Ones in Iraq and Afghanistan," *ProPublica*, September 23, 2010b. As of July 31, 2013:
http://www.propublica.org/article/this-year-contractor-deaths-exceed-military-ones-in-iraq-and-afgh-100923

Miller, T. Christian, and Doug Smith, "Injured War Zone Contractors Fight to Get Care," *Los Angeles Times*, April 17, 2009. As of July 31, 2013:
http://www.latimes.com/news/nationworld/nation/la-na-contractors17-2009apr17,0,5505250.story

Mission Critical Psychological Services, homepage, undated. As of September 25, 2013:
http://www.missioncriticalpsych.com/

Mojtabai, Ramin, "Americans' Attitudes Toward Mental Health Treatment Seeking: 1990–2003," *Psychiatric Services*, Vol. 58, No. 5, 2007, pp. 642–651.

Montreux Document on Pertinent International Legal Obligations and Good Practices for States Related to Operations of Private Military and Security Companies During Armed Conflict, September 17, 2008. As of September 25, 2013:
http://www.eda.admin.ch/psc

National Center for Health Statistics, *Health, United States, 2012: With Special Feature on Emergency Care*, Hyattsville, Md., 2013. As of August 28, 2013:
http://www.cdc.gov/nchs/data/hus/hus12.pdf

Nordan v. Blackwater Security Consulting, LLC, 382 F.Supp.2d 801, 2005. As of July 10, 2013:
http://www.pbs.org/wgbh/pages/frontline/shows/warriors/contractors/complaint.pdf

Office of the Deputy Assistant Secretary of Defense for Program Support, "Contractor Support of US Operations in the USCENTCOM Area of Responsibility to Include Iraq and Afghanistan," April 2013. As of July 31, 2013:
http://psm.du.edu/media/documents/reports_and_stats/us_data/dod_quarterly_census/dod_quarterly_census_april_2013.pdf

Office of the Under Secretary of Defense for Acquisition, Technology, and Logistics, *Acquisition Strategy for Defense Base Act Insurance: Report to Congress in Response to Section 843 of the National Defense Authorization Act for Fiscal Year 2009*, Washington, D.C., 2009. As of July 31, 2013:
http://www.acq.osd.mil/dpap/cpic/cp/docs/acq_strategy_defense_base_act_insurance.pdf

Pacella, Maria L., Bryce Hruska, and Douglas L. Delahanty, "The Physical Health Consequences of PTSD and PTSD Symptoms: A Meta-Analytic Review," *Journal of Anxiety Disorders*, Vol. 27, No. 1, January 2012, pp. 33–36.

Paykel, E. S., D. Hart, and R. G. Priest, "Changes in Public Attitudes to Depression During the Defeat Depression Campaign," *British Journal of Psychiatry*, Vol. 173, No. 6, 1998, pp. 519–522.

Pelton, Robert Young, *Licensed to Kill: Hired Guns in the War on Terror*, New York: Three Rivers Press, 2007.

Penn, David L., and Shannon M. Couture, "Strategies for Reducing Stigma Toward Persons with Mental Illness," *World Psychiatry*, Vol. 1, No. 1, February 2002, pp. 20–21.

Peralta, Eyder, "After Seven Years, Families of Slain Blackwater Contractors Settle Suit," National Public Radio, January 6, 2012. As of July 10, 2013:
http://www.npr.org/blogs/thetwo-way/2012/01/06/144804089/after-seven-years-families-of-slain-blackwater-contractors-settle-suit

Perkonigg, A., R. C. Kessler, S. Storz, and H. U. Wittchen, "Traumatic Events and Post-Traumatic Stress Disorder in the Community: Prevalence, Risk Factors and Comorbidity," *Acta Psychiatrica Scandinavica*, Vol. 101, No. 1, January 2000, pp. 46–59.

Phinney, David, "Adding Insult to Injury: Injured Halliburton Contractors Return Home to Fight Battle for Medical and Disability Coverage," *CorpWatch*, May 24, 2005. As of July 31, 2013: http://www.corpwatch.org/article.php?id=12286

Pietrzak, Robert H., Julia M. Whealin, Rebecca L. Stotzer, Marc B. Goldstein, and Steven M. Southwick, "An Examination of the Relation between Combat Experiences and Combat-Related Posttraumatic Stress Disorder in a Sample of Connecticut OEF-OIF Veterans," *Journal of Psychiatric Research*, Vol. 45, No. 12, December 2011, pp. 1579–1584.

Pratt, G. Michael, environmental science engineering officer, U.S. Department of Army, Combined Joint Interagency Task Force–435, "Air Quality Summary on Bagram Air Field (BAF)," memorandum, April 15, 2011.

Ramchand, Rajeev, Terry L. Schell, Benjamin R. Karney, Karen Chan Osilla, Rachel M. Burns, and Leah Barnes Caldarone, "Disparate Prevalence Estimates of PTSD Among Service Members Who Served in Iraq and Afghanistan: Possible Explanations," *Journal of Traumatic Stress*, Vol. 23, No. 1, February 2010, pp. 59–68.

Real Warriors Campaign, homepage, undated. As of September 25, 2013: http://www.realwarriors.net

Renshaw, Keith D., "Deployment Experiences and Postdeployment PTSD Symptoms in National Guard/Reserve Service Members Serving in Operations Enduring Freedom and Iraqi Freedom," *Journal of Traumatic Stress*, Vol. 23, No. 6, 2010, pp. 815–818.

Richardson, Lisa K., B. Christopher Frueh, and Ronald Acierno, "Prevalence Estimates of Combat-Related Post-Traumatic Stress Disorder: Critical Review," *Australian and New Zealand Journal of Psychiatry*, Vol. 44, No. 1, 2010, pp. 4–19.

Risen, James, "Contractors Back from Iraq Suffer Trauma from Battle," *New York Times*, July 5, 2007. As of July 31, 2013: http://www.nytimes.com/2007/07/05/us/05contractors.html

Rodriguez, Paola, Darren W. Holowka, and Brian P. Marx, "Assessment of Posttraumatic Stress Disorder–Related Functional Impairment: A Review," *Journal of Rehabilitation Research and Development*, Vol. 49, No. 5, 2012, pp. 649–666.

Rona, Roberto J., Margaret Jones, Nicola T. Fear, Lisa Hull, Matthew Hotopf, and Simon Wessely, "Alcohol Misuse and Functional Impairment in the UK Armed Forces: A Population-Based Study," *Drug and Alcohol Dependence*, Vol. 108, No. 1, 2010, pp. 37–42.

Rona, Roberto J., Margaret Jones, Amy Iversen, Lisa Hull, Neil Greenberg, Nicola T. Fear, Matthew Hotopf, and Simon Wessely, "The Impact of Posttraumatic Stress Disorder on Impairment in the UK Military at the Time of the Iraq War," *Journal of Psychiatric Research*, Vol. 43, No. 6, 2009, pp. 649–655.

Ruggiero, Kenneth J., Kevin Del Ben, Joseph R. Scotti, and Aline E. Rabalais, "Psychometric Properties of the PTSD Checklist–Civilian Version," *Journal of Traumatic Stress*, Vol. 16, No. 5, October 2003, pp. 495–502.

Scahill, Jeremy, *Blackwater: The Rise of World's Most Powerful Mercenary Army*, New York: Nation Books, 2007.

Schafer, J. L., *Analysis of Incomplete Multivariate Data*, London: Chapman and Hall, 1997.

Schell, Terry L., and Grant N. Marshall, "Survey of Individuals Previously Deployed for OEF/OIF," in Terri L. Tanielian, Lisa H. Jaycox, Terry L. Schell, Grant N. Marshall, M. Audrey Burnam, Christine Eibner, Benjamin R. Karney, Lisa S. Meredith, Jeanne S. Ringel, and Mary E. Vaiana, eds., *Invisible Wounds of War: Summary and Recommendations for Addressing Psychological and Cognitive Injuries*, Santa Monica, Calif.: RAND Corporation, MG-720/1-CCF, 2008. As of February 19, 2013:
http://www.rand.org/pubs/monographs/MG720z1.html

Schnurr, Paula P., Carole A. Lunney, Michelle J. Bovin, and Brian P. Marx, "Posttraumatic Stress Disorder and Quality of Life: Extension of Findings to Veterans of the Wars in Iraq and Afghanistan," *Clinical Psychology Review*, Vol. 29, No. 8, 2009, pp. 727–735.

Schooner, Steven L., and Collin D. Swan, *Contractors and the Ultimate Sacrifice*, Washington, D.C.: George Washington University Law School, Legal Studies/Public Law Research Paper No. 512, September 1, 2010. As of July 31, 2013:
http://ssrn.com/abstract=1677506

Schulz, Sabrina, and Christina Yeung, "Private Military and Security Companies and Gender," in Megan Bastick and Kristin Valasek, eds., *Gender and Security Sector Reform Toolkit*, Geneva, Switzerland: Geneva Centre for the Democratic Control of Armed Forces, United Nations International Research and Training Institute for the Advancement of Women, and Organization for Security and Co-operation in Europe, Office for Democratic Institutions and Human Rights, 2008. As of August 1, 2013:
http://www.unrol.org/files/GPS-TK-PMSC.pdf

Seal, Karen H., Thomas J. Metzler, Kristian S. Gima, Daniel Bertenthal, Shira Maguen, and Charles R. Marmar, "Trends and Risk Factors for Mental Health Diagnoses Among Iraq and Afghanistan Veterans Using Department of Veterans Affairs Health Care, 2002–2008," *American Journal of Public Health*, Vol. 99, No. 9, September 2009, pp. 1651–1658.

Security Association for the Maritime Industry, "Psychological Support for Private Maritime Security Companies," November, 2012.

Sié Chéou-Kang Center for International Security and Diplomacy, University of Denver, *Private Security Monitor*, online database. As of 2013:
http://psm.du.edu

Smith, Mark W., Paula P. Schnurr, and Robert A. Rosenheck, "Employment Outcomes and PTSD Symptom Severity," *Mental Health Services Research*, Vol. 7, No. 2, 2005, pp. 89–101.

Spearin, Christopher, "Special Operations Forces a Strategic Resource: Public and Private Divides," *Parameters*, Vol. 36, No. 4, Winter 2006, pp. 58–70.

Squires, David A., "Explaining High Health Care Spending in the United States: An International Comparison of Supply, Utilization, Prices, and Quality," *Commonwealth Fund*, Vol. 10, No. 1595, May 2012, pp. 1–12.

Substance Abuse and Mental Health Services Administration, *Results from the 2010 National Survey on Drug Use and Health: Mental Health Findings, Nsduh Series H-42, HHS Publication No. (SMA) 11-4667*, Rockville, Md., 2012. As of August 28, 2013:
http://www.samhsa.gov/data/nsduh/2k10MH_Findings/2k10MHResults.htm

Sundin, Josefin, Nicola T. Fear, Amy Iversen, R. J. Rona, and Simon Wessely, "PTSD After Deployment to Iraq: Conflicting Rates, Conflicting Claims," *Psychological Medicine*, Vol. 40, No. 3, 2010, pp. 367–382.

Thornicroft, Graham, Elaine Brohan, Aliya Kassam, and Elanor Lewis-Holmes, "Reducing Stigma and Discrimination: Candidate Interventions," *International Journal of Mental Health Systems*, Vol. 2, No. 1, April 2008, pp. 3–9.

U.S. Department of Defense, *Analysis of the Interim Report of the Commission on Wartime Contracting in Iraq and Afghanistan*, Washington, D.C., November 4, 2009. As of July 19, 2013: http://www.acq.osd.mil/dpap/pacc/cc/docs/TFWC_Rpt_to_USD.pdf

———, Office of Defense Procurement and Acquisition Policy, *FY12 DoD Services Contract Inventory*, 2012. As of July 31, 2013: http://www.acq.osd.mil/dpap/cpic/cp/acquisition_of_services_policy.html

———, Office of the Inspector General, *Health Care Provided by Military Treatment Facilities to Contractors in Southwest Asia*, Washington, D.C., May 4, 2009.

U.S. Department of Defense Instruction 6490.08, Command Notification Requirements to Dispel Stigma in Providing Mental Health Care to Service Members, August 17, 2011.

Vogt, Dawne S., Susan P. Proctor, Daniel W. King, Lynda A. King, and Jennifer J. Vasterling, "Validation of Scales from the Deployment Risk and Resilience Inventory in a Sample of Operation Iraqi Freedom Veterans," *Assessment*, Vol. 15, No. 4, 2008, pp. 391–403.

Wise, Jimmie I., *Outsourcing Wars: Comparing Risk, Benefits and Motivation of Contractors and Military Personnel in Iraq and Afghanistan (2009–2011)*, Monterey, Calif.: Naval Postgraduate School, 2012. As of August 1, 2013: http://www.dtic.mil/cgi-bin/GetTRDoc?Location=U2&doc=GetTRDoc.pdf&AD=ADA563459

Zajac, Andrew, "Halliburton, KBR Burn Pit Suit Thrown out by U.S. Judge," Bloomberg, February 28, 2013. As of July 31, 2013: http://www.bloomberg.com/news/2013-02-28/halliburton-kbr-burn-pit-suit-thrown-out-by-u-s-judge.html

Zatzick, Douglas F., Charles R. Marmar, Daniel S. Weiss, Warren S. Browner, Thomas J. Metzler, Jacqueline M. Golding, Anita Stewart, William E. Schlenger, and Kenneth B. Wells, "Posttraumatic Stress Disorder and Functioning and Quality of Life Outcomes in a Nationally Representative Sample of Male Vietnam Veterans," *American Journal of Psychiatry*, Vol. 154, No. 12, December 1997, pp. 1690–1695.